# ✴celtic magic

## essentials

# ✳ celtic magic

## *essentials*

james lynn page

## foulsham
LONDON • NEW YORK • TORONTO • SYDNEY

# foulsham

The Publishing House, Bennetts Close, Cippenham, Slough,
Berkshire, SL1 5AP, England

ISBN 0-572-02736-2

Copyright © 2002 W. Foulsham & Co. Ltd

Cover illustration by Jurgen Ziewe

Printed in England by Cox & Wyman, Reading, Berkshire

# Contents

# Introduction:
# **The Celtic Dawn**

*'A grove there was, untouched by men's hands from ancient times, whose interlacing boughs enclosed a space of darkness and cold shade, and banished the sunlight from above. No rural Pan dwelt there, nor Silvanus, ruler of the woods, no Nymphs; but gods were worshipped there with savage rites, the altars were heaped with hideous offerings, and every tree was sprinkled with human gore.'*

Lucan (first century AD)

On some windswept headland, on a tiny, remote Scottish island, a police officer from the mainland has arrived to investigate the disappearance of a child. Though these are the latter years of the twentieth century, the island is an eerie, sinister place somewhat at odds with the modern world. The first unusual thing a visitor would notice is the names of the residents: Oak, Willow, Alder, Ash, Holly and Briar. Here archaic pagan superstitions prevail over the 'civilised' Christian world: there are naked outdoor games, phallus-shaped topiary borders to the lawns, and lewd songs echoing from the public bar, the Green Man. Though the islanders seem friendly enough, the policeman realises during his investigations that they have something to hide. He suspects the child he is looking for is being deliberately hidden, being prepared as an offering to the people's gods.

Although he does not know it yet, he will end his days on this island, for he is still a virgin and has come of his own free will to this barbarous place. This makes him a perfect sacrifice for the islanders, who want to appease their goddess, who failed to provide a good crop the previous year. The policeman does find the girl, only to realise too late that he himself is the offering. He is 'the king that must die', the 'fool for a day' of pagan custom. He struggles as he is placed inside a colossal figure made of willow twigs. This is set alight and soon engulfed in flames as the goddess of the harvest receives her sacrifice. The islanders gather below the pyre and sing a cheerful song dating from the early thirteenth century, 'Sumer is icumen in'. They join hands and sway, giving thanks for next year's successful harvest.

In the next chapter you'll discover the significance of this scene. The book as a whole is a compact but comprehensive introduction to Celtic magic so, if you know nothing at all about the subject, this is the perfect place to start. And if you want to improve your own life with some Celtic magic, you'll find out exactly how to do so in Chapter 7.

# Chapter 1
# Long Ago on the Island of Brittia

*'Post war archaeological research has yielded a broad outline of what tribes were like in the era of the Druids, their customs and their level of primitive technology, but this evidence relates to the Celtic inhabitants as a whole. What we really seek is knowledge of the select band of priests who were important enough to be mentioned in the Greek texts – and it is at this stage that we encounter a difficulty.'*

Roy Norvill, *Hermes Unveiled*

S ome readers may have recognised in the Introduction the bare outline of the film *The Wicker Man*, which portrays a modern island community with its heathen values and beliefs still very much alive. The film was derived partly from Julius Caesar's *Gallic Wars* written in 55 BC. Certain editions of the book, inspired by Caesar's text, include a seventeenth-century illustration of a massive hollow figure in the shape of a man. Inside are victims about to die in a sacrificial pyre. The caption runs: 'The Wicker Colossus of the

Druids, Wherein Malefactors, Prisoners of War and Sometimes Innocent Persons were Burnt as Sacrifices to their Deities'. Caesar had witnessed the Druids in Gaul at first hand during his military activities, which ended with his conquest of them in 56 BC. Here is what he said:

*'... [the Gauls] judge that the only way of saving a man's life is to placate the gods by rendering another life in its place, and they have regular instituted sacrifices of the same kind. Some tribes have colossal images made of wickerwork, the extremities of which they fill with live men; they are then set on fire and the men burn to death.'*

There is only one thing wrong with this tale: it may not be true. Caesar is famous among scholars for describing the 'barbarian hordes' he conquered in as bad a light as possible, and a wicker colossus is an unlikely construction; it would have toppled over as soon as the lower parts were alight. So we should treat some of the texts by classical authors such as Caesar, Strabo, Posidonius and Tacitus with some scepticism. Unfortunately the surviving histories of the Celtic peoples of Europe and Britain were all written by these classical scholars. The broad accounts may be essentially factual, but details are often exaggerated. They are mostly tales of battles won for the Empire, and history is written by the victors.

There are no Celtic historians from the period to offer their side of the story, but as scholar Nora Chadwick points out, 'in their illiteracy the Celtic peoples were in no way remarkable. On the contrary, it is the literate peoples of the world who, at least until recent times, have been relatively few in number'. Nor did learned Celts, the Druids and bards, write down their teaching and knowledge, so we have no first-hand accounts of, for example, their religious practices. Their knowledge was the result of divine inspiration: the secrets were then transmitted orally through people trained in memorisation techniques. So our earliest reliable sources for the lifestyles, beliefs and culture of the Celtic people came from archaeology.

## The Celts in Britain

As the first Indo-European people to spread across Europe, the Celts (from the Greek *keltoi*) emerged in the south-central part of the continent in about the fifth century BC, arriving on British shores, first in Ireland, a century later. They came from Gaul (modern France) and possibly belonged to a larger group of people called the 'Pretani', from which we eventually arrive at the word 'Britain'. (The writer Pytheas refers to the Pretanic Islands.)

Before the Roman occupation of Britain, theirs was a society skilled in the arts of iron working. This produced agricultural tools for farming and husbandry, weapons for war and pottery and exquisite metal workings for decorative and practical purposes. Casear had made a half-hearted incursion into Britain in 55 BC (and another the following year) to find it populated by a large collection of tribes. The country was divided into separate kingdoms without any political unity. There was a widespread population of tribes such as the Belgae, Dumonii and Cantiaci along the south and south-west coast, the Trinovantes and Iceni lived in East Anglia, and in the north, in an area roughly from south of Hadrian's Wall to modern Cheshire, tribes included the Brigantes, Carvetii and Parisii.

Of those in south Britain Caesar writes:

*' … by far the most civilised inhabitants are those living in Kent whose behaviour differs little from that of the Gauls. Most of the tribes in the interior [i.e. not on the coast] do not grow corn but live on milk and meat, and their garments are skins.'*

The comparison is made with the Gauls here because they are known to have developed a society of extraordinary sophistication. So we find that:

*'... the ground is densely studded with dwellings, closely resembling those of the Gauls, and a great number of cattle. For money they use either bronze, or gold coins or iron ingots of fixed weights. Tin is found inland, and ... as in Gaul there is timber of every sort, except beech. Hares, fowl and geese they do not think it lawful to eat, but rear them for pleasure.'*

The dwellings Caesar describes are likely to have been large circular structures with conical roofs; together with other structures they would have formed a kind of farmstead. Had Caesar ventured into Ireland, however, he would have found no coinage. There the means of trade was barter with cattle. The reason why this idyllic, pastoral existence continued in Ireland is precisely because the Roman military machine never got that far.

Whether Caesar intended any permanent conquest of Britain is not known, though the journey yielded plenty of logistical knowledge for possible future invasions. He realised, for example, that since Britain was divided into separate kingdoms, each could be attacked separately. The *modus operandi* would be to overcome tribal chiefs and then force their allegiance to the Empire: each would be installed as a 'client king' (such as happened with the later Herods in first-century Palestine) and granted Roman citizenship. The newly subjugated, Romanised Celtic kings would therefore feel unable to rebel, and would not ally themselves with Celtic kingdoms that had not yet been conquered. As their reward, these puppet kings would be patronised and protected by Rome: they would receive titles and enjoy the lifestyle and privileges of any other high-status Roman official. There was one woman, however, who was having none of this.

## The pride of the Celts: nature and beliefs

In the early years, Camulodonum was ruled by the wealthy Cunobelinus, whose name means 'the hound of the god of war'. In AD 40, three years after Cunobelinus's death, the Emperor Claudius invaded Britain and the kingdom became known as Colchester, a place that would figure strongly in the Romanisation of Britain.

Later, however, Colchester was destroyed by rebels in a bloodbath: its Roman occupants, including children, were slaughtered without mercy and its temple burnt to the ground. Dio Cassius, a third-century historian, records that the person who carried out the carnage was a woman 'enormous of frame, terrifying of mien, and with a rough shrill voice. A great mass of bright red hair fell down to her knees; she wore a huge twisted torque of gold, and a tunic of many colours.'

This is the famous warrior queen Boudicca, the widow of Prasutagus, king of the Iceni, who had ironically colluded with the Empire as one of its client kings. When Prasutagus died, the Roman officials acted with great arrogance, refusing to recognise the independence of the Iceni (such as it was) and seeking to make it a territory of the Empire. When Boudicca complained and asserted her right to leadership, the Romans had her flogged and her two daughters were raped.

The Iceni rose up in revolt with the neighbouring Trinovantes and, with the military commander Suetonius Paullinus and his soldiers occupied elsewhere, the destruction of Colchester began in earnest. In the final battle, however, the superior Roman military machine shattered Boudicca's rebellion. She drank poison rather than be taken prisoner.

The Roman writer Tacitus says that before the final battle, Boudicca made this brave speech to rally her forces:

> *'We British are used to women commanders in war ...*
> *But now I am not fighting for my kingdom and wealth.*
> *I am fighting as an ordinary person for my lost freedom,*
> *my bruised body, and my outraged daughters ... the gods*
> *will grant us the vengeance we deserve.'*

It is unlikely that these are the actual words of Boudicca (for where is Tacitus's eyewitness source, about 50 years after the event?) but they do echo the perceived qualities of her bravery in battle. Dio Cassius agrees, saying that when Boudicca 'grasped a spear it was to strike fear into all who observed her'.

Fierce as the Celtic tribes were in war (Caesar observed that they dyed their bodies with woad, presumably to make them look more terrifying), they failed to organise themselves into any national or political unity and so failed to achieve success.

Despite racial similarities, there was a thick strain of independence running through the Celtic psyche, hence local tribal gods may be found in one region but not another. This individual pride can also be seen in the Celtic way of dressing, and Dio Cassius's description of Boudicca wearing a 'tunic of many colours, over which was a thick mantle held by a brooch' reflects what we know from archaeological evidence about the Celts' dress and appearance, especially their love of personal decoration.

*The Snettisham Torc*

Physically, Celts seem generally to have had a tall, strong build, with long faces and blue eyes, topped with blond or auburn hair. They apparently took especial care with their hair. Strabo says: 'they continually wash their hair with lime wash and draw it back from the forehead ... with the result that their appearance resembles that of the Satyrs of Pan'. Again in Strabo we find, 'ornaments of gold, torques on their necks and bracelets on their arms and wrists, while people of high rank wear dyed garments sprinkled with gold'. He adds that, 'it is this vanity that makes them unbearable in victory and so completely downcast in defeat'. (Elsewhere, we find that the

Celts are 'driven headlong by their passions, and never submit to the laws of reason'.)

Perhaps this notion of 'vanity' – or at least the high value placed on personal appearance – is not inaccurate given the archaeological discovery of a very ornate looking glass, known as the Desborough Mirror. The many archaeological finds from Britain and the continent reveal not only the Celts' love of beauty, but also their fine craftsmanship: along with bronze torques and collars, there are fibulas (a kind of safety pin) made of silver gilt, necklets, chains, bone hair combs, chatelains (belt-like chains) and pairs of armlets ending in snake's heads. Many of these have been recovered from grave excavations, so they also offer clues to the Celts' spiritual beliefs.

Sepulchral goods were often buried with the dead to accompany the person on his or her journey to the afterlife. One of the more significant examples comes from a dig in Hochdorf, a village in southern Germany. A burial chamber, dated to about 550 BC, was discovered containing a large bronze bier decorated with scenes for a ritual dance; beneath it were fixed eight female figures on wheels. It resembled a long metal couch on eight ornate casters. On this 'couch' was a Celtic chieftain, who had been laid to rest dressed in silks and garlanded with flowers, with his grave goods of gold brooches, nail clippers, a wooden comb, a golden dagger and shoes, the latter decorated with strips of gold. In the external chamber more funerary goods were found, one of which has great significance for the mythic elements of the Celtic world: it was a bronze cauldron, amazingly still bearing traces of sediment from the honey mead it once contained. The cauldron, as we shall see, is a recurring motif in the Celtic tradition as a vessel containing the magical properties of regeneration, abundance and immortality.

There is further archaeological evidence for this belief in the so-called Gundestrup Cauldron, a bowl made of silver dating from the first century BC. It is – like most Celtic art – highly stylised and decorated with peculiar hybrid creatures among stags, dolphins and what appear to be wild boar. It also depicts a military procession: a line of soldiers standing in a row, each waiting to be plunged into a cauldron in a ceremony of mystic renewal. Also depicted is a squatting humanoid figure; in his right hand he holds up a torque, in his left a serpent with a ram's head. This is Cernunnos, the Lord of the Animals (whom we shall meet again later), a precursor of any mythic 'wild man of the woods', closely related to nature deities like the Greek Pan or Roman Silvanus.

Cernunnos

This is a rare example of Celtic art that depicts an actual physical form. Most often found are sweeping tendrils, whorls, spirals and curlicues. As one commentator, Paul Jacobsthal, puts it: 'The repertory is narrow; the image of man is limited to huge menhir-like statues in stone, in bronze to a few busts or miniature doll-like men and a multitude of heads. There are very few natural animals; most of them are fantastic and highly stylised'. Jacobsthal goes on to say, significantly, that 'ambiguity is a characteristic of Celtic art' because it is essentially poetic. He says 'to the Greeks a spiral is a spiral and a face is a face … whereas the Celts always "see" the faces "into" the spirals'. However, among the free-flowing abstractions and mythical creatures, one can glimpse the artists' intention: one of symmetry and harmony.

This is obvious, for example, in the patterns on the Desborough Mirror and the Witham Shield, and in the Lindisfarne Gospels and the many examples of Celtic knotwork: they are representations (in the modern sense) of the patterns of energy that lie behind the manifest universe and, as such, emanate from a common 'divine' centre, secretly connecting all forms of life to each other. Viewed in this light, the Celtic art that Paul Jacobsthal says lacks concrete form is no mere decoration, but is a means of representing the ephemeral, fluid and spontaneous aspects of life. In the case of the later Christianised knotwork designs, with their skilfully interwoven lines and curves, often appearing as if in relief out of a dark background, we can see a vast array of endlessly interlocked energy patterns. This is how the modern physicist would describe the ultimate nature of the universe, and such patterns – irrespective of their use by Christian monks – are based on the occult principle that regards the perfect square as symbolising the manifest universe, and how the One at the centre is reflected in the Many.

As for the earlier Celtic metalworker, it is important to state that he was given a very high status as he set to work with iron, silver or bronze. This artist of the forge was there to merge the natural with the supernatural, representing the innate 'wholeness' of life with its symmetries and abstractions, the source of Life expressed in its many different 'shapes'. The painter Cecil Collins expresses the idea in this way:

*'There was a time when artists were employed to set up altars to the gods of Life … Beneath our technological civilisation there still flows a living river of human consciousness within which is concentrated in continuity the life of the kingdom of animals, plants, stars, the earth and the sea, and the life of our ancestors, the flowing generations of men and women … the secret inarticulate longing before the mystery of life.'*

Collins adds that 'the artist is a vehicle for the continuity of that life' and it is in this respect that the Celtic smith was more magician than metalworker.

## The Druids

*'So Suetonius planned to attack the island of Mona, which although thickly populated had also given sanctuary to many refugees ... The enemy lined the shore in a dense armed mass. Among them were black robed women with dishevelled hair like Furies, brandishing torches. Close by stood Druids, raising their hands to heaven and screaming dreadful curses. This weird spectacle awed the Roman soldiers [at first] into a sort of paralysis ... [finally] Suetonius garrisoned the conquered island. The groves devoted to Mona's barbarous superstitions he demolished. For it was their religion to drench their altars in the blood of prisoners and consult their gods by means of human entrails.'*

This account, by the Roman Tacitus, of Suetonius Paullinus's attack on Mona (modern Anglesey) in AD 61, explains why Boudicca was free to sack Colchester. But what of these 'barbarous superstitions' and bloodlettings? Such 'pagan' practice seems to contradict the more cerebral, spiritual pursuits that Caesar describes in his *Gallic Wars*:

*'A lesson they take particular pains to inculcate is that the soul does not perish, but after death passes from one body to another ... They also hold long discussions about the heavenly bodies and their movements, the size of the universe and of the earth ... and the power and properties of the gods; and they instruct the young men in all these subjects.'*

The Druids, with their mystical rites and their image as guardians of impenetrable, arcane wisdom have excited much comment ever since classical writers like Strabo and Caesar first drew our attention to them. They have been described as 'priests', 'high magicians', 'astronomers', 'wizards' and 'prophets', though the source of the word Druid reveals its symbolic meaning. The word seems to be a combination of the Greek word *drus* (oak tree or oak wood) and the Indo-European infinitive *wid* (to know). Thus, a Druid is 'one who knows the oak': not very enlightening until you realise the totemic power and sanctity of the oak tree in Druidic thinking. As Frazer points out in *The Golden Bough*:

*'... the Druidical belief, reported by Pliny, was that whatever grew on an oak was sent from heaven and was a sign that the tree had been chosen by the god himself. Such a belief explains why the Druids cut the mistletoe not with a common knife, but with a golden sickle, and why, when it was cut, it was not suffered to touch the earth.'*

Pliny says the Druids 'choose oak woods for their sacred groves and perform no sacred rites without oak leaves'. With its great age and size, the oak represents everything that speaks of life, that is enduring and immortal, and it was the Druids' task to interpret the handiwork of the gods in all forms of nature. In fact, all the names listed to describe the functions of the Druids would be applicable and we can infer that they were teachers of what we might call occult or hidden knowledge. In the Druid colleges, Caesar tells us, the initiate might spend up to 20 years learning the secrets of nature, which would encompass anything from natural lore (herbs and plants), to astronomy, philosophy and law. It is important to stress that the Druids would not have seen these subjects as separate: all are manifestations of the One principle.

In more intellectual areas like the law (we are told by Caesar that the Druids acted as judges in all kinds of disputes), the powers of reason and impartial logic required would be seen as not so much issuing from within, but as divinely bestowed. In the same way the night sky was seen as an emanation from the gods, just like the power of the mistletoe, which in winter – as the host tree's leaves disappear – remains full of divine, fruitful life. The mysterious presence of the gods is to be found everywhere, in nature and human reason as much as in the stars and planets.

Mistletoe, much used in Druidic ritual, grows not from the ground but high up in the oak's branches, and gains a golden-yellow hue months after it has been cut down. It is associated with Virgil's mythic Golden Bough, with its 'flickering gleam of gold. As in the woods in winter cold the mistletoe – a plant not native to its tree – is green with fresh leaves and twines its yellow berries around the boles; such seemed upon the shady holm-oak the leafy gold, so rustled in the gentle breeze the golden leaf.' The mistletoe is imbued with magical properties,

an emanation of solar fire, the universal healer the Druids cut down with their golden sickles. According to Pliny, 'they believe that a potion prepared from mistletoe will make barren animals to bring forth and that the plant is a remedy against all poison'.

The mistletoe or Golden Bough is an early symbolic motif of divine power and light (or wisdom) that appears in later myths in different guises such as the Grail or the Philosopher's Stone of the alchemists. We shall encounter this reverence among the Celts for magical objects with life-bestowing properties again. What of their secret teachings, however? How much can be accurately inferred from a people who did not write down their knowledge? The way in which Caesar describes the Druidic system resembles the continental mystery cults of ancient Greece, but closer still, it resembles the organisation of mystical first-century Jews known as the Essenes. The historian Josephus tells us that they officiated in public trials, believed in the immortality of the soul, swore not to reveal the secret teachings to outsiders, and 'in their anxiety to cure disease they learn all about medicinal roots and the properties of stones'.

Scholars have long noted the distinctly 'un-Jewish' qualities here – the doctrine of the soul, herbalism and crystal magic (indeed, Josephus himself says that the Celts taught the ideas of the 'sons of Greece') – but it is the following line about this communal sect that is the most tantalising: 'To people outside the silence within seems like some dread mystery.' In much the same vein, the modern author Frank Delaney says of the Druids:

Celtic magic

*'Mystery, their energy, gave them the means of gaining and
retaining power ... In a rural society, the man who interpreted
the elements, who had access to the gods, held power.'*

This, like the aura surrounding the Druids, is where their
power lay: they possessed secret knowledge to which ordinary
outsiders were not privy.

If the Druids were 'people who knew the oak', however, this
can only mean that they had penetrated its mystical secret, for
this 'knowledge' is *gnosis*: knowledge not merely of external
things but of the Self and its proper relationship to the world,
its cycles and rhythms, how it 'fits' into the overall scheme of
the universe. The gold-yellow mistletoe, the shimmering
Golden Bough, symbolised enlightenment and the wisdom
gained from great age, just as in later Celtic myth Merlin
outlives the oldest oak tree, so becoming the wisest man of all.

If there was any 'mystical secret' to uncover, however, it was
related to the Oneness of the Universe (literally, 'the one
turning'): that what is 'out there' has some mysterious
connection with what is 'in here', so that divine 'occult'
knowledge was accessible under certain conditions. This paints
the Druids as magicians, and though their role was often
patristic (relating to the early Christian theologians) and
priestly, it was their function to interpret the signs of the gods
for ordinary folk. As I have stated, knowledge of any kind,
including ideas leading to practical inventions, would be seen as

a gift from the gods: it was specialised, esoteric ('for the few'), sacred knowledge that lay with people like the Druids. As Plutarch says, 'secrecy even increases the value of what is learned'.

On the subject of secrets and beliefs, Mircea Eliade writes that:

*'... the cultural value of "secrecy" has as yet been inadequately studied. All the great discoveries and inventions – agriculture, metallurgy – implied, in the beginning, secrecy, for it was only those "initiated" into the secrets of the craft, who were believed to guarantee the success of the operation.'*

We have seen how the Celtic smith, in the execution of his art, was essentially dealing with the divinely symbolic world, but this applied just as much to the actual metals he worked with. As the spiritual quest of the alchemist, for example, led to the establishment of modern chemistry, the Celtic metalworker would have been viewed as a kind of thaumaturge (wonder worker), helping to create new forms in nature. Mircea Eliade again:

> *'As for the metallurgist, he accelerated the "growth" of ores, he made them "ripe" in a miraculously short time ... [fashioning] a different thing from what already existed ... This is why, in archaic societies, smelters and smiths are held to be masters of fire, along with shamans, medicine men and magicians.'*

I leave the Druidic sacrifice of victims in a wicker colossus for others to argue about. Regarding the unusual Druidic rite (in Pliny) of removing the sacred mistletoe with a golden sickle at night, Professor Stuart Piggott finds this 'inexplicable'; moreover, the mention of mistletoe as a 'universal healer' is to be treated with circumspection (the plant has a reputation for being poisonous). However, viewed symbolically, it becomes something quite different. Some commentators have seen this rite as an allegory for the achievement of divine knowledge through the process of meditative introspection. As Roy Norvill says:

'... *having discovered the inner meaning of the "oak" symbol [the eternal Self] there can be little doubt that the "druid" who worships at it is merely another name for the initiate ... the sickle, by its shape, represents the Moon ... a symbol of reflection.*'

The oak groves, he adds, are 'the "oak groves" of their own minds'.

# Chapter 2
# Ancient Gods, Ancient Wisdom

The true life of nations, it has been said, is the life of the imagination: that is, beneath a country's administrative and political machinery, its laws and institutions, lies the 'sense of place', the mythic idea of a nation.

In the case of Britain, for example, the 'heritage industry' promotes the romantic notion of 'Britishness' (and all that it implies) amid the rosy glow of Albion's past. Organisations like the National Trust touch upon the unconscious notion of a long-gone Arcadia: the charm of places like the Lake District, a despoiled abbey or a ruined castle, the romance of stone circles and hill forts, any environment of ancient beauty that nourishes the imagination. In such places – a village, meadows full of sheep, tumbling brooks, places of cliché and poetry – we can almost sense a previous Eden-like existence.

There is magic in the landscape, and this mystical sense of engagement with the environment, this romantic sense of place, is a peculiarly Celtic attitude. As author Michael Bracewell comments, 'there is a need within the psyche of Englishness to look back to an idealised past', but as we shall see in Celtic lore,

31

this is not a new phenomenon. During the medieval period, when most of the legends were written down, authors were already reminiscing about the former glories of Albion.

There is no clearly defined starting point in Celtic myth for the legends of our idealised past, however. The gods and goddesses do not spring from one major source or 'family' like the Olympians of classical Greece. As the writer R.J. Stewart points out, there is really no 'formal unity or pantheon of Celtic gods and goddesses' because the sources of the tales are many and varied, and differ from place to place. The stories were also written (or, at any rate, compiled) at different periods of history. Such is the case with the 'biography' of King Arthur. Supposedly a British chieftain or king in the sixth century, his story is not covered in depth until the early twelfth century. Later contributors to the Arthurian saga combine other elements – the Round Table and Sir Lancelot, for example – not found in the earlier traditions. Since the earliest Celtic lore was not written down, it is often difficult to infer just what elements of the later literary tradition were part of this 'authentic' oral transmission.

When interpreting Celtic myth, it is therefore more useful to look at its repeated motifs and recurring themes, as if there are only a few archetypal ideas or universal patterns (concerning gods and goddesses, heroes, kingship, nature and cosmology) that continually reappear in different guises, with a change of name. There are certainly no early extant images of Celtic deities, and the ones dating from the Roman period are a product of classical influences. It is said that when the Gaulish military leader Brennus attacked Delphi, he was amused to find carvings and idols of the Greek gods represented in the form of human beings. To the Celtic mind, the divine could never be faithfully represented by some material object fashioned by a human being. Perhaps this gives us our first clue to the Celtic world view.

## 'The folk of the God whose mother is Dana': the Goddess

You may prefer their better-known epithet, the 'Tuatha dé Danaan', a people who according to one legend came to Ireland 'out of heaven'. In another they 'went to the northern islands of the world learning Druidry and knowledge and prophecy and magic, until they were experts in the art of pagan cunning'. Dana, the ancient patroness of the Irish gods, is a primal Mother Goddess. Though very little is recorded about her, a localised Irish deity, Anu, is associated with her and the 'Paps of Anu' of County Kerry in south-west Ireland are named for the goddess. (In Wales her name was Don, and her children provided the names for certain astronomical phenomena.) The genesis of the Tuatha dé Danaan is in the union of the Morrighan and the Daghda, broadly speaking the 'feminine' powers of Darkness and the 'masculine' powers of Light. (In one version Dana is the Daghda's daughter; in another she is identified with the Morrighan.) Both are often patron-like figures, on hand to offer protection and guidance to their people.

The Morrighan presides over mortality; she can bestow life or take it away, and is often shown in early lore as a figure of sexual allure or as an embodiment of horrible rage, who could transform herself into fearful shapes and turn men against each other. She was also a prophetess, however, whose foresight helped the Tuatha dé Danaan in battle. She also appears as the Triple Goddess, identified by scholars with the three phases of the moon: waxing, full and waning. This cycle is, in turn, symbolically connected to the Maiden/Mother/Crone archetypes, phases of the Feminine, like the Greek three-headed Hecate. This sequence could also be called Birth/Fruitfulness/Death.

The Goddess

From earliest times, the power of the Feminine was the dominant force in the minds of the Celts, with the emphasis on Darkness and Night, and the hidden and innate mystery contained there. For it is with all that is Feminine that we are closest to the source of Life: we are born of our mother's womb, a place of darkness, and during her pregnancy we are one flesh with her. She is the life giver, then the nourisher and provider, and this experience is imprinted deeply upon our unconscious. That the Morrighan is a symbol of fate and mortality is no surprise, for as Carl Jung states:

*'… the Indo-European root mer or mor, means "to die" … With the Celts the conception of the Fates probably passed into that of the matres and matronae, who were considered divine by the Teutons … May it perhaps point back to the great primordial image of the mother, who was once our only world and later became the symbol of the whole world?'*

The Great Mother is also synonymous with the earth itself, the land. Whether seen in natural features like hills (breasts), caves (vagina) or the river that, in one legend, results from the Morrighan urinating over the land, such images are the primary stuff of life. In the same way, just as we are born of matter and flesh, we return to the earth in death. These 'given facts' of human existence are why the Feminine force in nature is associated with Fate, in its many guises. Death is, of course, the ultimate Fate, as when the Morrighan appears as a raven, a traditional symbol of death, on the shoulder of the dying Irish warrior-hero Cuchulainn.

One aspect of this Triple Goddess is Brighid. In her virginal form she is related to the Greek Athene (another virgin), the patroness of artisans and weavers, who teaches handicrafts to humankind. Her Roman name is Minerva, the goddess of cultural development, arts and science, and in medieval literature she appears as the muse for the poet Taliesin. The theme we see here is one of inspiration and enlightenment: indeed, she was the goddess of the Brigantes tribe of northern England, where she was known as 'Brigantia', meaning 'bright' or 'exalted one'. As the Queen of Heaven who hangs her cloak upon the sun's rays, she was celebrated at the Celtic fire festival of Oimelc or Imbolc on 31 January, when the dark days of winter are coming to an end. (Significantly, the start of the Celtic year was Samhain, 1 November, when the blackness of winter is approaching.)

With the coming of Christianity she became Bride or St Brigid. In one myth she is midwife to the infant Jesus, and wears a headdress of lighted candles; she places three drops of spring water upon the Divine Infant's brow. (This legend is based on the earlier Celtic theme of a Son of Light, whose wisdom is bestowed by the goddess.) Bride's association with childbirth here is in her in role as the matron, the second lunar phase of fullness, fecundity and completion. Here she is the provider, the 'giving goddess', as when she attempted to establish a monastery at Kildare. A rich landowner had promised her the land, then foolishly attempted to deceive her by allowing only as much land as her cloak would cover. Being a goddess, however, and wise to the duplicity of humans, she cast her cloak ensuring it covered many miles of countryside.

Other Sons of Light born to the goddess appear elsewhere in Celtic myth. In the *Mabinogion,* the Victorian name given to the collection of early Welsh literature from medieval times, we find Rhiannon, a goddess who appears on earth to mate with mortal men, and whose golden-haired child is the subject of a dark mystery. He disappears, only to be raised elsewhere until his true identity is recognised. Fostering also appears in the story of the goddess Arianrhod, the daughter of Don (Dana), whose 'fine, chubby, yellow-haired boy' is raised into youth by Gwydion, Arianrhod's magician brother. However, it is the goddess who presides over the boy's fate: 'I lay this destiny upon him, that he shall never have a name until he receives one from me.' She also puts two curses upon the boy: that he shall never bear arms, and that he shall never have a wife until Arianrhod decides it. However, by gentle deception, the boy finally manages to gain his name, Llew, and arms; his wife is magically created from the blossoms of the oak, broom and meadowsweet, and is called Blodeuwedd.

We are back to the power of the Feminine: Arianrhod, whose name means 'silver circle' or 'queen of the wheel', is identifiable as the lunar 'night force', the Unconscious energy that binds the individual to his or her destiny, to that part of one's life that cannot be changed – in other words, fate. Arianrhod is both the goddess who places the curse upon Llew and the figure through whom it is removed. However, to gain his name, his arms and his wife, he must 'deceive' the goddess. In the modern sense, and especially in a magical context, Llew symbolises the proper relationship of ego to Unconscious, for this 'gentle deception' is one way of getting it to yield its gifts. Llew persuades the goddess of things that are essentially untrue; when believed by her, they become true. Students of magic may see echoes here of techniques used in auto-suggestion and visualisation: they are based on the occult law that any magical intent or idea must first be accepted or 'believed' by the Unconscious (as already true) if the magic is to work.

In a more obviously helpful guise Arianrhod appears as the Greek Ariadne, who helps Theseus escape from the Labyrinth by using a long piece of thread. This is also the thread of life spun by the Three Fates, as Erich Neumann says:

*'The primordial mystery of weaving and spinning has also been experienced in projection upon the Great Mother who weaves the web of life and spins the thread of fate, regardless of whether she appears as one Great Spinstress or, as so frequently, in a lunar triad.'*

We meet with this Great Spinstress in the early Irish myth of the Tain Bo Cuailgne (the 'Cattle Raid of Cooley'), when Queen Mave sees a mysterious maiden with a face of rich blood, who holds 'a weaver's sword', and who declares that her intention is to 'reveal thy chances and thy fortunes'. She may be identified with the Red Lady who later declares her love for the warrior Cuchulainn. Exhausted from battle, he declares her appearance untimely; she responds by saying she will give him assistance and protection in any deed he undertakes. When he still refuses her help she becomes angry, saying that from now on she will hinder everything he does. When he lunges after her with his sword she changes into a black crow, for the enigmatic Red Lady is, in fact, the Morrighan in disguise.

So there is an inherent paradox in these Great Mother archetypes, who first offer their love and then taunt the hero with obstacles that sometimes lead to his death. We meet her in modern life too, and psychology describes her in terms of projection on to the Terrible Mother, the devouring Feminine aspect of life. For example, we encounter this darker face whenever we come across an 'unfair' and often irrevocable 'fate' with its accompanying emotional pain and humiliation, which no amount of reasoning can assuage. This may be an extreme example but it is quite common; the 'unfair humiliation' is a sign that the ego must genuinely realise its own smallness and impotence in the greater drama of life, if anything is to change. For it is only through the Goddess that we can, to borrow a mythical metaphor, 'reclaim the kingdom'. Great suffering can be relieved only by real acceptance, forgiveness, patience, faith and (to an extent) gentle insight and self-understanding, all attributes of the Goddess's more positive face. Only by 'letting go' can we become healed.

Not surprisingly then, the power to heal is another attribute of the dark goddess Morrighan, called Morgan Le Fay in later Arthurian tradition. Despite her continual persecution of Arthur, it is she who is on hand to receive the wounded hero on the Island of Apples; she declares that his health will be restored if he stays with her for many days, making use of her healing art. In modern life, however, such 'bad fates' and humiliations usually appear wherever there is blindness and ignorance, particularly when we have complacently believed we are invincible and immune to defeat. If 'pride goes before a fall' it does so only because the Unconscious seems to 'engineer' such events, for the Goddess will not allow us to become any more than we truly are.

## Gods and heroes

The goddesses of the Celts seem to be embodiments of our fate: the irrevocable unfoldings of the Unconscious that seem to have a pre-destined quality, marking out boundaries for the hero. Their masculine representations in nature therefore depict the 'solar' half of the psyche, that which seeks consciousness. Though this is true of all hero myths, the Celtic gods are somehow different. Though we meet with many epic battles and the weary struggles of warriors, in Celtic lore there is never any real sense that 'might is right' as with, say, the Roman Mars or the evil Set of Egyptian myth. In the case of the Tuatha dé Danaan, their weapons of war are magical spears, invincible swords and the power of invisibility to outwit the enemy. As T.W. Rolleston points out:

*'... the Danaans represent the Celtic reverence for science, poetry and artistic skill, blended ... with the earlier conception of the divinity of the powers of Light. In their combat with the Firbolgs the victory of the intellect over dullness and ignorance is plainly portrayed ...'*

This emphasis on higher, more spiritual forces is widespread in other male figures of Celtic myth: in Taliesin, the great bard/prophet; in Merlin and the noble Arthurian knights; in the god-king Bran who sacrifices himself to a more worthy cause by asking that his men decapitate him, so that his head may become a source of oracular wisdom and physical sustenance.

Indeed, the chief masculine archetypes of Celtic legend are not bloodthirsty, power-mad figures bent on conquest; they are prophets, wise men, shamans, smiths or wounded kings who need the help of a noble youth in order to redeem the country.

Even one of the very earliest Celtic gods is no vengeful Father in the manner of the Hebraic Yaweh or the Greek Cronos, but is almost a figure of amusement. The Daghda, chief of the Tuatha dé Danaan (whose epithets are 'Father of All' and 'Lord of Perfect Knowledge') wielded a huge magical club, so heavy it required at least eight men to lift it. For his amusement he would slay his nine attendants simultaneously with one end of his iron staff, and with the other bring them back to life. He was enormous, with an equally huge appetite, the cause for a grotesquely comic episode when his enemies, the Fomorians, test him with a superhuman feat. They provide porridge and gallons of milk, which they pour into a massive pit together with whole sheep, pigs and goats, insisting that he eats

The Turoe stone

everything. Not only does he eat it all (with a spoon big enough for two people to lie in) but continues to gorge on the earth and gravel below. Then he mates with one of the Fomorian women, who is so delighted with his sexual performance that she turns her own magical strengths on her own people. He also possesses a cauldron with the power to work miracles, which later becomes one of the four treasures the Danaans bring with them into Ireland. Each comes from one of the four wondrous cities: Falias, Gorias, Finias and Murias. From Falias comes the Lia Fail, the Stone of Destiny; from Gorias the invincible Sword of Lugh of the Long Arm; from Finias a magic spear; and from Murias the Cauldron of the Daghda, which would leave no one unsatisfied. (These four objects – stone, sword, spear and vessel – are obviously an early version of the four Tarot suits, which we shall meet again in the Arthurian myths.)

Despite the Daghda's physical capabilities for war and conquest, his coarse eating habits and sexual athleticism, he is also a skilled harpist and a wise patrician who leads by example; his more common title is the 'Good God' (that is, 'good at everything'). His more crudely comic aspects presumably belong to an earlier strand of tradition, and perhaps have survived because they portray the ideal image of Celtic masculinity: sheer physical energy that is channelled into fatherly concern for his relatives, and into artistic and creative skills.

We see something similar in the Irish god Oghma who, though demonstrating martial prowess, is also a god of the intellect and learning. Indeed, it is he who invented the Celtic alphabet known as Ogham script (more of that later). However, if we turn to the Welsh tradition we do find a figure who at first suggests the darkness of uncontrolled rage and the powers of evil. His name is Gwyn ap Nudd, a warrior who is also the Prince of the Dead and whose domain is the Underworld. According to Rolleston, he 'glories in the crash of breaking spears', gathering together the souls of dead heroes in his Underworld realm. There is also an echo of the Greek Hades abducting Persephone in an episode where Gwyn steals a bride-to-be, Creidyladd, and carries her off by force. Arthur, however, secures her release on condition that the prospective groom, Gwythyr, fights for her each spring with the dark Lord of the Dead. Yet *gwyn* is an old Welsh word meaning 'fair' or 'white', so Gwyn is, confusingly, also a god of light. This paradox is resolved, I feel, in the ancient poem 'The Black Book of Carmarthen', where Gwyn declares that he has witnessed much spilling of blood, having seen great heroes like Arthur and Bran fall to their deaths as the ravens screech, and whose helmet is now broken 'by the thrusting of spears':

> *'I have been where the soldiers of Britain were slain,*
> *From the east to the north:*
> *I am escort of the grave.*
> *I have been where the soldiers of Britain were slain,*
> *From the east to the south:*
> *I am alive, they in death.'*

Contrary to what Rolleston suggests, this sounds more like a sad lament for the passing of great men; Gwyn is nothing more than a force of nature, a personification of death on the one hand and, on the other, the guide of souls, escorting the brave to the Great Place Below. Rather like Milton's Lucifer (meaning 'light bearer' and formerly the Hebrew Satan) in *Paradise Lost*, Gwyn is also a god of light. No sight is now too shocking; no spilt guts on the battlefield will turn his stomach. In other words, through his intimate encounter with one of nature's great irrevocable forces, death (of which he is also the instrument, presumably because the hero's time has come), and through knowing at first hand the suffering of mortals, he has come to sympathise with their plight (just as our own human pain makes us more sensitive to it in others). Though he cannot die himself, he is sick of war, complaining of the 'torment of battle', and in so identifying with the mortal world he has gained some understanding of it. He knows what pain means to human beings; in short, he has become enlightened. That Gwyn belongs primarily to the powers of Light is also expressed in the universal metaphor where darkness, when it has finally exhausted itself, must turn into its opposite, light.

Now we consider Lugh of the Long Arm, whom we met briefly as the Welsh god Llew. He is youthful, handsome and brilliant and, like the Daghda, is a 'good god'. He is skilled, versatile and fully deserving of his title, Samildanach, the 'many gifted one'. As a youth he is made head of the magical

Otherworld until he reaches manhood, and returns from there bearing marvellous gifts. One is the Boat of Mananan, son of the sea god Lyr, which possessed the ability to know the thoughts of men, and would at once bear its rider wherever he wished. Lugh appears one day to offer his services at Tara, the royal palace of Nuada of the Silver Arm, the reigning king of the Danaans. The doorkeeper asks him what useful services he can provide; Lugh says he is a skilled carpenter. When told there is already a master carpenter at court, Lugh declares that he is also a smith; he is rejected once more since they already have one. Lugh then lists all the many arts and skills in which he is accomplished – poet, bard, harpist, metalworker, physician, scientist, magician – only to be told that men of creativity and knowledge possessing each of these skills are already in residence. Lugh's reply is a master stroke: 'Then ask the king if he has in his service any one man who is accomplished in every one of these arts, and if he has, I shall stay here no longer.' Naturally Lugh is admitted to the court, and hence is known by the surname, Ildanach the 'all-craftsman'.

There are unmistakable parallels here with the precocious Hermes of Greek myth, the messenger god who, like his Roman counterpart Mercury, presides over communication, particularly the art of divination, the secret language of the gods. So Lugh is not merely a symbol of gifted youth, or a symbol of light over darkness (his name means 'light' or 'shining one'), for all the many skills he possesses have their origin in magic, in divine inspiration. They are powers dispensed only by the gods themselves. Poetry, for example, in the Celtic world was also a form of prophecy; the smith or metalworker, through smelting, magically created new forms from the raw stuff of the world; musical skill was likewise divinely inspired; scientific knowledge was less about quantity than quality. In other words, the essence of the universe was not a set of external weights and measures, but a spiritual quality, whether in stars, planets, stones, trees, men or women: each contained something of the gods' intentions. To say that Lugh possesses these gifts is also to say that he symbolises them and, as such, he is a kind of allegory for human growth, knowledge and development.

Historically, this tradition was overseen by the Druids, whose oral teachings were nothing less than the kind of divine knowledge we have been discussing. As Nora Chadwick puts it: 'In societies ignorant of books and the written word all knowledge is regarded as a spiritual possession and acquired by spiritual means or "inspiration".'

One episode involving Lugh, when he avenges the death of his father, who had been killed by the three sons of Turenn, exemplifies the Celtic ideals of valour, heroism and honour. Instead of seeking revenge through their deaths, Lugh sets them several almost impossible tasks. At one point, Lugh casts a spell over the brothers, so they temporarily forget to obtain the penultimate treasure, a golden cooking spit from the bottom of the ocean. The last task results in a battle where they are mortally wounded. Only Lugh's magical pig-skin will heal and save them, but he refuses to hand it over, causing the death of the three sons. In the final analysis though, Lugh achieves his ends, not through bloodlust, but with cleverness, wit and guile. He sits back and watches his enemies destroyed in the quest he has himself initiated. (That Lugh, being a divine youth, may have foreknown the ultimate fate of the three brothers is not usually considered by scholars.)

Whether one sees see this tale as symbolising the outwitting of brute force by skilled intellect or merely as the triumph of good over evil, it forms part of a larger Celtic theme where, as we have seen, the powers of the mind and its ability to retain knowledge were highly prized. Not only knowledge, but also verbal skills, the honey-tongued power to charm and enchant, were also valued: in short, the power of the spoken word. We are back to the poet/bard Lugh here; to the persuasive tongued Hermes/Mercury; and, in particular, to the Celtic god Ogmios, a native of Gaul, who is depicted as an old man dressed in a lion's skin, with seven disciples in tow, their ears attached to his tongue by tiny gold and amber chains of great delicacy and beauty. He represents the force of eloquence, the power of creative language (via the imagination) to shape and influence the world. Whether this means the magician's incantatory spell or the carefully chosen words we use every day to affect others' lives, the source is the same: the god of eloquence. This is a million miles from the image of the Celtic warrior as the naked, woad-smeared yob of the classical writers. As Stewart asserts:

*'There is ample evidence that [the Celts] were sophisticated and complex people, far indeed, from the notion ... that they were barbarians or savages until the Romans marched in to civilize them at the point of a sword.'*

# Chapter 3
# The Coming of Merlin

Myths are the stories we tell ourselves to give meaning to the chaotic, the unpredictable. They are our attempt to make known the unknown, to explain reality through the power of image and symbol. Mythographer Joseph Campbell says, for example:

> '... it would not be too much to say that myth is the secret opening through which the inexhaustible energies of the cosmos pour into human, cultural manifestation. Religions, philosophies, arts, the social forms of primitive and historic man ... the very dreams that blister sleep, boil up from the basic magic ring of myth.'

The major themes found in Celtic myth are much the same as in any other and as such transmit a rich vein of symbolic 'truth' about the world. While the historian and anthropologist may view the deeds of legendary deities as personifications of nature, with its unending cycles and occasional, unpredictable terrors, the psychologist has found much there to be a metaphor for the outpourings of the human Unconscious. The mythological symbols are therefore symbols for the life of the soul itself. The unknowable forces of the Unconscious appear as the dark underworld of Hades, Tartaros or Purgatory; its powers are inimical to the light of the conscious mind, a place where different rules apply. Then there is the place we might lose ourselves: the frustrating Labyrinth, the depths of the Dark Forest. These are places where no human belongs: a sub-aquatic grotto or the undergound cave, the abode of the Three Fates.

These are places the hero, the ego, must encounter: they are the trials consciousness itself must undergo. A huge effort is usually required to obtain something of great value; a perilous quest is involved to recover a precious object that cannot be won without undergoing great personal danger. In Celtic myth these obstacles may be even subtler, such as the stupidity or disloyalty of a companion: Arthur is cuckolded by the unfaithful Guinevere and her lover, Lancelot. (Such 'dishonourable' deeds can have drastic consequences.) The chief motif is the still the quest, however, and in many Celtic stories the object of the quest is a magical vessel of some kind, like the Magic Cauldron of Cerridwen, the Grail, or the ever-full Daghda's Bowl, objects that confer personal riches, special gifts or even immortality. The colour gold often appears in Celtic tradition, in man-made objects or clothing, but whatever precious objects arise, these 'treasures' are always the unsuspected and hidden properties of the Unconscious. In the end, mythic gold and riches are the same as those sought in the laboratory of the Alchemist's soul, a state of spiritual perfection transmuted from the base matter of earthly life. This, then, is the Quest for the Holy Grail, the real 'treasure hard to attain', best expressed in the powerful story of the Grail knight, Parzival, whom we shall meet in the following chapter. Standing behind this mythical quest is the fascinating and ambivalent figure of Merlin.

The popularised image of Merlin is of a wizened, white-bearded magician with a robe, wand and cone-shaped hat. His original incarnation was nothing of the sort, however. Our first recorded knowledge is from 1136 with the publication of the *Historia Regum Brittaniae,* supposedly a bona fide history of the British kings by Geoffrey of Monmouth. Geoffrey tells us

Maiden Castle

he was not the originator of this work, but merely a translator and editor of a very ancient book. It reads like a combination of myth and history, however, with legendary elements woven into the structure. Furthermore, it is clear that Geoffrey used extant Welsh poems attributed to Myrddin, a sixth-century bard. In the allegedly genuine history, we first meet Merlin in the fifth century at the court of the devious King Vortigern, who is worried about an impending invasion from the Picts in the north. The Saxons have already made inroads into Britain, and Vortigern retreats into Snowdonia to erect a defensive retreat. The building of the castle gets under way, but is found to have mysteriously collapsed the following morning. Vortigern summons his magicians, who tell him that to counter this malign force he must find a youth 'who had never had a father'; and when he had found him, he should kill him and sprinkle his blood over the mortar and stones. This, they said, would make the foundation of the tower hold firm.

In time, such a youth, called Merlin, was found by Vortigern's messengers in Camarthen. He was brought to the court accompanied by his mother, who tells the court of his curious birth: she conceived Merlin after being visited by 'someone in the shape of a handsome young man' who then 'suddenly vanished'. A court attendant identifies this mysterious being as a spirit that resides 'between the moon and the earth': it is an incubus, who is 'partly human, partly angelic'. As a result of this union between a human and an otherworldly being,

Merlin was born almost full grown and able to speak straight away. He was also covered in hair, humorously dramatised in Nikolai Tolstoy's *The Coming of the King*:

*'From my neck to my feet I was covered with a beautiful soft pelt of brown hair ... still wet and sticky from the place where I had lain snug for so long ...'*

His three midwives reacted in horror, one saying to the attendant priest that the child must be the offspring of the Evil One. And so the newborn begins his dignified reply: 'Look here, madam ... '. Precocious indeed but, as we have seen, eloquence is a special gift in Celtic tradition and signifies a form of higher wisdom: Merlin is, in fact, a prophet.

When Merlin later asks Vortigern why he and his mother have been summoned to court, the king explains his exasperation over the construction of the castle. Merlin replies that the foundations are unstable because of two dragons sleeping beneath a pool there, ready to fight one another. Merlin gives a long prophetic utterance about what the dragons symbolise: the Saxons will be temporarily victorious, but the Britons will defeat them, and one day the son of Uther Pendragon, Arthur, will come to the British throne. Naturally, his predictions come true.

In another significant episode recounted by Geoffrey in his *Vita Merlini* (and in the anonymous *Life of St Kentigern*) we see Merlin in the guise of the shaman, the figure who, by going

Merlin

beyond the limits of everyday consciousness, receives visions and prophecies from the gods. Here Merlin is overcome by grief at the warring kingdoms of the day, how they lead to death and the spilling of blood. Then, 'after he had filled the air with all his lamentations, a strange madness seized him and he stealthily slipped away. He fled to the woods, unwilling to be observed in his flight, and entered the forest', living on 'the fruits of trees', making friends with the animals, for 'he became a wildman, as though he had been born in the woods'. Here, in the forest of Calidon (southern Scotland), he would continue his days 'concealed like a wild beast'. In time, his sister Ganieda (wife of King Rodarchus, king of the Cumbri tribe) sent servants to the forest to find Merlin. He is returned to the king's court and promised gifts if he will stay. Merlin rejects this offer, and the king has him bound in chains, for it is now clear to everyone that he is a madman.

At this time Merlin predicts the Threefold Death, as a test of his supposed powers of prophecy. In a pre-arranged situation, he is introduced to a particular male youth whom he says will die by falling from a high rock. A second youth, with shorter hair, is then brought before Merlin. The prophet says he 'will meet a terrible death in a tree'. Finally, a 'young woman' is summoned, and Ganieda says: 'Come brother, tell me how this virgin will die.' Merlin replies: 'Whether virgin or not, "she" will die in a river.'

Merlin has not been fooled – he knows all three are the same person – but how can the same person die in these three different ways? As the youth reaches manhood, he falls down a mountainside in a hunting accident. At the foot of the mountain is a tree; his foot catches in a branch and the rest of his body is submerged in the river below. Thus did 'these three perils prove the prophet right'. In a different version of the tale it is Merlin himself who dies in this way: 'Pierced by a stake, suffering by stone and water, Merlin is said to have met a triple death.'

The Threefold Death is a common mythic theme, appearing in the tale of Lleu (Lugh), who dies on a riverbank, pierced by a spear. This recalls the Teutonic Odin, who is 'hung on the windswept tree for nine full nights, wounded with a spear'. Tarot students will recognise this as the image that has survived in the Hanged Man card, traditionally symbolising a kind of voluntary sacrifice to fate. It relates more specifically, however, to a renunciation of the material, the worldly, in 'exchange' for spiritual rewards or knowledge, just as Merlin refuses the gifts of King Rodarchus in preference for the life of the wilderness.

The parallel with Jesus on the cross, who is pierced by a spear resulting in a flow of blood and water, is hardly accidental, since the Gospels contain as many pagan ideas as they do Judaeo-Christian ones. As Nikolai Tolstoy writes: 'The self sacrifice of god is accompanied by symbols, Tree, Spear and Water, whose significance can only be guessed at.' If we introduce the cup that caught the drops of blood as Jesus hung on the cross, we have the four represented elements: the realms of matter (tree), spirit (blood), soul (cup) and mind (spear). In other words, this transformation is accompanied by the vital forces of Life, or the four major elements necessary to it. In psychology this is called the process of Individuation, a term coined by Jung for the arrival of psychic 'wholeness', a point of potential maturity and integration in a human life, which has been preceded by many trials and lessons (symbolised, of course, by the struggle of the mythical hero).

## Merlin the magician

It should be clear by now that among its symbolic themes Celtic myth contains broad hints of what might be called mystery or initiatory teaching, with Merlin, a kind of composite figure, embodying the attributes of the archetypal Wise Man. Thus far, I have made no mention of the more familiar elements of the Merlin legend in Geoffrey's *History*: the sword in the stone, the institution of the Round Table, Avalon or the Holy Grail. It was a poet from Burgundy, Robert de Boron, who introduced these features in the early thirteenth century. Here we recall again the New Testament figure of Jesus, for de Boron's Merlin is a figure whose resemblance to the life of Jesus is made quite plain. Born of a virgin and an otherworldly spirit, Merlin is sought out by an evil king (Vortigern) who wants to put him to death. Later he becomes a renowned prophet, disappearing into the wilderness to seek union with divine forces. Both Jesus and Merlin undergo a death with ritualistic undertones. The theme of the divinely inspired being, born of a virgin, also occurs in the Persian myth of Zoroaster, whose precociousness parallels that of Merlin. Merlin could speak fluently soon after birth; Zoroaster laughed out loud as soon as he was born.

As we have seen, Merlin, the seer and prophet, half human, half divine, lives in both the civilised, conscious world, and in the uncivilised realm of the forest, the Unconscious. This makes him a powerful symbol for the shaman-magician. He is an archetype embodied in every modern magical spell or invocation, in all properly executed 'positive thinking'. He represents the ability to 'enter' and embody the world of the Unconscious, the occultist's astral realm of Imagination, and to return to the conscious world of ordinary, external appearances. He returns with new powers, however.

In his role as a sorcerer, one Merlin episode requires little serious interpretation. Through his magical art, he is credited with transporting the menhirs of the 'Giant's Dance' from Ireland to England; hence the appearance of what is now called Stonehenge on Salisbury Plain. Though this feat drew criticism from Merlin's enemies, such as King Lot, who called it 'the devil's craft' and Merlin a 'faytoure' (impostor), I cannot think of a more colourful metaphor for Jesus's 'faith can move mountains'.

The Castlerigg Circle

One of the better-known magical feats over which Merlin presides is the removal by Arthur of the magical sword Excalibur from the stone, to prove his worthiness to assume the throne. In Celtic mythology stones were often associated with ancestral spirits, so there is a loose connection with royal lineage here, but I feel its real symbolism lies in the realm of magic. As we have seen, the symbolic Sword has survived in the modern Tarot deck: it represents the powers of the mind and its awakening, what writer Tom Chetwynd calls 'the sharp steel of the spirit'. It represents the emerging consciousness of the Hero, who is being separated from what Chetwynd terms 'the state of being mother bound'. At this point the Hero must undertake the quest ahead, with all its potential pitfalls, with uncertain courage. Viewed in a more magical sense, however, and taking Merlin-Arthur as two halves of the same process, it is a symbol of heightened awareness (or magical powers of will) beyond the confines of the 'lowly' material world. The stone, we may say, represents the crystallised habit patterns and the limitations of matter; Merlin is the tutelary Wise Old Man who inspires the Arthurian Quest that must follow. The departure point is the removal of the Sword, the raw but potent energy of the mind: it is the gift of awareness, the clear truth that cuts away illusion, the creative power of thought itself with its new ideas and inspirations.

There are further New Testament echoes in de Boron: he had already composed a verse epic about the legendary Joseph of

Arimathea and the story of the Grail as the cup used by Christ at the Last Supper. Here the Grail's ultimate destination is 'in the vales of Avaron (Avalon)'. De Boron's poem of Merlin seeks to explain how the Grail travels from Palestine to Britain, and later mentions Merlin establishing a Fellowship of the Round Table at Carduel (Carlisle) for 50 knights. By the time Sir Thomas Malory's *Le Morte d'Arthur* was published in 1485, the number of knights had reduced to 12, a significant 'magic' number of completeness. The Fellowship swear an oath consisting of a code of honour, propriety, and fair play, 'every year … at the high feast of Pentecost'. (This celebrates the moment the Holy Spirit descended upon Jesus's disciples.) That there should be parallels between Arthur and his 12 knights and Jesus and the 12 disciples is no accident: the material was written in the Age of Chivalry, when story-book knights were imputed with the requisite Christian virtues.

It is Merlin, in his guise as magical patron, who creates the Round Table Fellowship. The very appearance of a Round Table that seats 12 chivalrous knights is, of course, rich with symbolic ideas: the common motif of the circle represents an entire cycle of events. It is eternity, something without beginning or end, an unbreakable union of oneness implied, even, in the traditional wedding ring. The circle stands for all human life and the energies inherent within it, for that is cyclical too. Twelve, on the other hand, is rooted in Antiquity as a sacred solar 'male' number, found in both the Old and New Testaments (12 tribes of Israel, 12 disciples), in Greek mythology (12 Olympian gods) and in the zodiacal signs derived from the 12 seasons. The zodiac wheel has been helpfully described by astrologer Robert Hand as 'a map of the psyche': the symbolic circle shows the fundamental energies of life, the 'map' we must navigate on our round journey of beginnings and endings.

## Merlin: dweller on the threshold

I discussed earlier the image of Merlin as the prophet of the wild who, because of his madness, becomes wise. His mystical embrace of entire humanity makes him completely ego-less (he 'loses his mind'); what results is total one-ness with nature itself, hence his power to prophesy the Threefold Death. I will now explore more fully this 'wild man' figure, embodied not only by Merlin but by figures such as the Horned God and Pan of classical mythology. They all combine in the idea of a nature god, a spirit of the woodlands, all that we now call 'pagan'. They symbolise the wild, unpredictable aspects of nature's power, which is why Christianity later sought to equate woodland deities like the Greek Pan with the Devil. Merlin, in Geoffrey of Monmouth's *Life of Merlin*, is depicted as the Lord of Animals; he bears a pair of stag's horns upon his head and is 'a naked madman, hairy and completely destitute'.

We see at once that the figure of Merlin is contradictory: there are mythic themes simultaneously associated with Christ – the prophet's hairy pelt even parallels the hair shirt of

The Lord of Animals

medieval monks – and the Devil. The latter connects us with the horned deity, Cernunnos, the Celtic god of hunting, and though Merlin cannot properly be described as a 'nature god', his power to command wild beasts shows he embodies the skills of the 'noble savage'. This figure has identified with and learned the ways of woodland denizens; he derives his spiritual powers by denying himself the comforts of civilisation. We are back with the figure of the shaman, who transcends the limits of the five senses and normal consciousness through either physical deprivation or some mind-altering substance (usually, the very plants he finds in the wild). Now he enters the Otherworld (through archetypal images arising from the Unconscious) and the powers of the spirit are made available to him, hence his ability to foretell the fates of kings.

We have seen how this 'strange madness' seized Merlin before his disappearance into the forest. It followed a period of fasting ('for three long days he wept, refusing food'), a technique known to the Celts for inducing shamanic ecstasy and trance-like visions. This was also associated with 'shape-shifting'; the traditional shape-shifter not only turns up in various human or animal forms, but can move in either direction in time – now a babe in arms, now a youth, now a very old person. The shape-shifter's shamanistic 'travel' is, of course, a psychological journey; its premise can be understood in the modern concept of 'energy' (in both psychology and particle physics) as the essential 'component' of life, being inherent in all things. In other words, the atomic particles that make up humans, animals, birds, trees, cars and skyscrapers all share the same nature. Moreover, this world of diffuse energy that lies beneath the world of forms is synonymous with the energies of the Unconscious mind: the realm of malleable, creative potential used by the magician. Shape-shifting can be viewed as another striking metaphor for the magical process in general: as energy manifesting itself in different forms or thoughts 'turning into' physical reality.

Merlin's appearance as the Wild Shaman who inhabits the wood leads us to another profound symbol: the forest itself, the dark realm of the Unconscious. As writer Ruth Padel puts it:

> *The forest stands both at the edge of town, full of brigands and wild animals, and at the back of the mind: European myth's great metaphor for where and how we are in life – alone, uncertain, losing and finding ourselves, each in "another part" of tangled darkness.'*

Continuing with this theme, scholar Heinrich Zimmer asks:

> *What is the world to the forest? What is conscious to unconscious? That is a question only Merlin can ask, which only he can answer … The answer is that he allows the forest, the abyss, to swallow him back, and he becomes again the magic wood and all its trees.'*

In other words, Merlin's withdrawal to the forest, his charting of the territory of the Unconscious, makes him a totemic figure who is the 'knower' of nature and the processes and vicissitudes of the physical world. That also means our physical world – the very lives we live, the setbacks we must encounter on the path, 'losing and finding ourselves' – and we benefit from having some kind of guide through this 'dark forest', the unknown. However, we also create our problems from ignorance of our true nature, which brings me to a related Merlin archetype, the Tarot's unprepossessing image of The Devil.

Essentially card number 15 of the Major Arcana is a Christian overlay of the wild Greek god Pan, with his goat's head and human body. This, in turn, is a later version of the Celtic horned god Cernunnos, or Shakespeare's Herne the Hunter. Its original divinatory meanings invoke the usual roll call of wicked deeds or bondage to sexual impulses. Arthur Waite, however, also calls it the Dweller on the Threshold Outside the Mystical Garden of Eden, that is, a figure at work in the psyche of humankind, marking out the boundaries beyond which we cannot go, reminding us of our human limitations, and that a meaningful, happy life requires some effort at self-mastery. In Waite, this card also means 'that which is predestined but is not for this reason evil', in other words, a card of Fate. Perhaps a painful one, too, but one for which the individual cannot escape some responsibility. This is often the problem for, faced with a painful experience, we would usually rather blame someone or something else instead of our own stupidity, vanity, jealousy, greed or malice.

However, in R.J. Stewart's excellent *Merlin Tarot,* the Devil has become The Guardian; it depicts Merlin as Lord of the Animals, with his stag's antlers. Here Merlin as the Dweller is 'a power that cuts away illusion' though, of course, the extent to which we are wrapped up in illusion or ignorance about ourselves determines the extent to which we will make a mess of our lives. Presumably this is why Stewart also equates this card with Purification, that is, purifying oneself of ignorance.

This requires an increase in understanding and an effort to change, but how are we first to acquire this raised understanding of the self, this knowledge of the total psyche? The short answer is probably through pain. Like the astrological Saturn, the Dweller is often a symbol of pain and limitation, for this is often the only way in which human beings not only learn, but learn the rules of the game that is Life.

That life's lessons (painful or not) have traditionally always been regarded as possessing inestimable value is portrayed in the language of alchemy: humankind is the 'crucible' in which 'base matter' is purified and transformed into gold. So Merlin as the Dweller is a teacher of wisdom, since to know oneself and the effect one has on the world (or what we receive back as Fate) is to also know how the universe works. Conversely, to paraphrase the physicist Werner Heisenberg, whenever we examine the world, instead of finding an objective reality, we always 'encounter ourselves'.

It is perhaps ironic, too, that these archetypes that prefigure human enlightenment and the dawning of wisdom are themselves portrayed as sad, alienated outsiders. In the early Welsh figure of Myrddin ('wandering with madness') we find the bard in the guise of a martyr, a persecuted seer, rejected and cast out by his own people. It is a common motif: the visionary prophet, misunderstood by his contemporaries, a scapegoat for the fears of common humanity. Indeed, hairy and ugly Pan (like the hairy and ugly infant Merlin), whom the other gods hated, nevertheless was the originator of Apollo's prophetic art and inventor of the Pan pipe, with which the sun god would make beautiful music. Similarly, the lowly, parasitic mistletoe, plucked from its formidable host, the oak, becomes the gleaming, magical Golden Bough; the spurned and rejected figure of Myrrdin, in the end, offers much of value to humanity. His wisdom is partly, of course, a condition of his seclusion and madness; through his descent into the dark forest of the Unconscious he has seen and understood things the rest of civilisation cannot. However, it follows that there is no real place for this kind of shaman in modern society. Astrologer Liz Greene says:

*'Only the man who has seen the vision … who has glimpsed the seven circles of heaven and the seven circles of hell, is free of meaninglessness. And most of these men can do nothing for the rest of us because they are mad.'*

## Chapter 4
# The Coming of Arthur

*'The acts of Arthur are the deeds of the giant Albion.'*

William Blake

There are at least three versions of the figure of Arthur. First, the popular one: the chivalrous, noble hero of the court of Camelot, the king of the Britons, who, identified with his magic sword Excalibur, gathers at the Round Table with his knightly companions. There is also the sometimes less than heroic and certainly flawed Celtic king brought to us by medieval writers. Then there is the 'real' Arthur: the historian Nennius, writing *c.* AD 800, writes of a Romano-Celtic chieftain named Artorius born in about AD 470, whose major claim to fame seems to have been to have repelled the invading Saxons during the sixth century. He was a warrior, skilled in the arts of metalwork and armour making, who enlisted the help of other cavalrymen in an attempt to fend off the Saxon foe. It is his name rather than any detailed account of his actions from this period that has survived.

Whether or not this is the source for the later transmitters of Celtic legend is a moot point, despite the claim by modern enthusiasts to have discovered archaeological evidence leading to this individual. We are dealing here with myth: ancient storytellers recounting epic deeds, stirring battles and heroic voyages were not historians in the strict, modern sense. They were compilers and transmitters of ancient oral tradition, keeping alive the power of mythic story-telling for its own sake. Much the same can be said of Geoffrey of Monmouth, whose near-contemporaries misunderstood this, and called him a 'writer of lies'. Geoffrey remains our fullest literary source for the character of Arthur (and of Merlin) and, though his tales were heavily Christianised, they can be seen as having distinctly Celtic themes.

In his *Historia Regum Brittaniae,* Geoffrey gives the beginning of Arthur's reign as AD 505. Following the death of his royal father, Uther Pendragon, he assumes the throne, armed with his 'unconquerable valour, learned tongue ... clear judgment and strong right hand'. Arthur leads his soldiers to victory against the Irish and the Scots and successfully conquers Iceland; news of such triumphs then 'strikes fear into distant kingdoms. Germany is alarmed, Gaul fortifies its walls, Rome trembles.' Yet the brave and chivalrous king, because he is mortal, must die (appropriately) on the battlefield. At one level, however, this is where his real story begins. For he is the Wounded King of myth, who can only be redeemed by the appropriate actions of a certain noble seeker on the Path.

In Malory's *Le Morte d'Arthur*, Merlin takes the young Arthur to a castle where his upbringing is entrusted to Sir Ector. Following the defeat of Arthur's father by the Saxons, Merlin gathers the knights of the court together for the test that will become the removal of the Sword. As we have noted, the 'once and future king' passes the test, establishing his worthiness to assume the crown. Later, though, since Arthur is headstrong in war and seeks revenge on King Pellinore, he suffers serious injuries and Excalibur breaks in two. He is thus both physically and spiritually vanquished, and waits in a hermitage for his wounds to heal. (It is significant, too, that Perceval, one of the Grail knights, will come from Pellinore's line.) After three days, Merlin takes the wounded Arthur to a magical lake:

*'... and in the middle Arthur was aware of an arm clothed in*
*white samite, that held a fair sword in that hand.*
*"Lo", said Merlin, "yonder is the sword that I spoke of."*
*So with that they saw a damsel going upon the Lake.'*

This is the Lady of the Lake, who tells Arthur that the sword belongs to her. However, if he will give her a gift when she asks him, Excalibur will be restored to him. Arthur replies: 'By my faith I will give you what[ever] gift ye will ask.' As Gareth Knight puts it, this event symbolises the way in which 'the heart and will is broken by its own ineptitude and in that condition of humility and repentance opens itself to higher spiritual forces

The Lady of the Lake

and aspirations'. Indeed, it is only when the futile efforts of the ego have been renounced, when we have ceased striving to exert control, that the powers of the Unconscious (its healing and life-giving aspects) come into play. For we need not look at this mythic episode, in which Arthur finally sacrifices his will to something greater, in a broad spiritual sense. Quite often, when the channels available to the forces of will and enterprise are blocked and our goal (whatever it may be) seems to elude us, it is this act of renunciation, this 'letting go', that provides the solution. Jung called this phenomenon the 'absolute knowledge' of the Unconscious, and when it emerges it seems possessed of magic. In any magical work undertaken to achieve a specific goal, a certain amount of trust is required, a faith in the magic itself, if the objective is to be fulfilled.

The gift the Lady of the Lake asks for is the head of Balin, the Knight of Two Swords, who has killed King Pellas (not to be confused with Pellinore, though both figure as slain kings). The central theme here is that the king is spiritually at one with the land. In a simple sense, his powers are, of course, the powers of the nation, its identity and strength, but they are also a spiritual factor, for without him the land is impotent. This theme is seen in the whole Arthurian cycle, where king and land can be restored only through the healing power of the Holy Grail.

## Parzival and the wounded king

The broad outline of the Grail quest can be described thus: a young, untutored knight must undertake a perilous quest. He finds himself in an enchanted castle where an old, wounded fisherman lives, and where various mysteries are shown to him. When he enters the castle the hero sees two youths carrying a mighty lance that is dripping with blood; later he sees two maidens carrying a large salver that bears a man's severed head (in Celtic legend these, together with the Sword and the Grail, are known as the Four Grail Hallows). Only by asking the question 'What does all this mean?' can these things, which bear the odour of injury and death, be avenged.

These are the bare bones of the narrative found in the ancient Welsh romance *Peredur,* whose eponymous knight comes from Arthur's court. In a later account, Chrétien de Troyes' *Conte del Graal* (*c.* 1180), Peredur has become Perceval, and the salver or platter is now a 'graal' that emits a bright, wondrous light. The day after he sees the mysterious vision of the salver he is chided by a maiden who tells him that, had he asked the meaning of what he had seen, the lame man (the fisherman) would have been restored to life. He was, in fact, the king. Perceval is also upbraided by a hideous-looking woman, who also curses him for not asking the question that would have restored the kingdom, for now maidens will be shamed and knights will die in battle, resulting in even more widows and orphans. That Chrétien died before completing his work (before Perceval

Perceval and Galahad

could return to the castle of the Fisher King) itself bears the hallmark of myth; one must engage with the mystery and divine its meaning oneself!

However, a later version of the Grail-king story, the medieval poem *Parzival*, written in 1200 by the German Minnesinger Wolfram von Eschenbach, has even richer symbolic layers. Possibly the most 'enlightened' version, it tantalises the reader with hints of mystical codes to be deciphered, that there is more than meets the eye:

> *'He who seeks to gain instruction from this tale must not*
> *wonder at the contrary elements brought to light therein ...*
> *If he sits not overlong, neither errs in his steps, but*
> *understands, then only will he reach his goal.'*

I shall return to this mystery element later. In Wolfram's story, Parzival is brought up in the forest by his widowed mother (again the theme of the hero's ambiguous conception). He leaves her in order to fulfil his male destiny, after seeing five knights ride by in gleaming armour; she dies full of mortal grief.

In one of his first adventures, though untutored in warfare, he kills the Red Knight and puts on his armour. Parzival then helps a young woman in distress: he makes love to her, but abandons her to continue his journey. He later sees a raven lying dead on the snow, which is stained with its blood; it reminds him of his lover's black hair, white skin and red lips. These symbols are the three spiritual stages in the process of alchemy: the black nigredo of the undifferentiated pysche in its base condition; the purifying 'whiteness' of approaching illumination as the dross is removed; and the redness of the sun, the goal, the enlightenment of wisdom. In other words, Parzival, though he does not know it, is undertaking a spiritual journey.

Then he meets a fisherman who tells him the way to the Grail castle. The castle magically appears before his eyes; there the sick Fisher King waits for him. Inside the castle a squire presents him with a sword that cannot be broken except in one perilous situation. Parzival sees figures bearing a white lance dripping with blood, two burning candelabras, the silver platter and the radiant Grail. He also sees an injured old man. All this means nothing to him, however, so he goes to bed. The next morning he wakes to discover the Grail castle is deserted and sets off to find his host, but as soon as he crosses the drawbridge the castle vanishes from sight.

The old man in a black cap, reclining on a couch the previous night, was, of course, the Wounded King, whose injury (depending upon which version you read) was in the groin or thigh. Whether or not this is an allusion to castration and the removal of procreative power, the wound itself is significant: it is both a sickness of the spirit and what makes the 'world' wither and die. This is portrayed in Eliot's poem, *The Wasteland*, as it asks 'what are the roots that clutch, what branches grow out of this stony rubbish?'; it contains images of 'lilacs out of the dead land' and 'that corpse you planted last year in your garden'. In this desolate state, nothing can grow, because the king's wound is reflected in the land. As Jean Houston says:

*'… an abundance of sacred wounding marks the core of all great Western myths … all of these myths of wounding carry with them the uncanny, the mysterious, the announcement that the sacred is entering into time.'*

It is this sense of the 'sacred', of something 'other', some sublime experience that turns around our lives, that is both a blessing and a curse, for often it cannot happen without the 'wounding'. Like the painful experiences of restriction symbolised by Merlin as the Dweller on the Threshold, Houston comments that:

*'... as seed-making begins with the wounding of the ovum by sperm, so does soulmaking begin with the wounding of the psyche by the Larger Story.'*

In other words, this is a sense of personal myth, the 'numinous', the sense that such occurrences are pregnant with meaning. Whether we are wounded by love or any of the many other experiences that plunge us into pain, it is only through a sense of a greater pattern underlying our life that in the end the experience may have some educational value, that we may finally find some meaning in it. As I discussed in the previous chapter, it seems that human wisdom is not to be gained without a 'wounding' of some kind, as Jung put it, 'by the unflinching exertions of a human being'. To understand this process, this Pattern, is also to understand our Path, our Destiny, whose seeds we carry deep within us. In the end, Parzival is able to heal the kingdom by asking the right question: 'Whom does the Grail serve?' His quest to 'find himself' thus begins by his asking 'What does all this mean?'

## The quest for the Grail

The symbol of the Holy Grail, though having its roots in Celtic lore, assumes its more familiar associations in the Christianised, medieval Grail legends. In de Boron's *Joseph d'Arimathie* (*c.* 1200) we learn how Joseph managed to acquire from Pilate the cup used by Christ at the Last Supper, then used it to catch the drops of blood of the crucified Jesus. Another text, *Le Grand San Graal,* tells how Joseph and his company finally arrive in Britain, bearing the Ark of the Grail. It is this legendary account that has resulted in certain attempts to discover the 'real' Grail: I recall a television broadcast in which a woman solemnly declared that a worn wooden chalice she owned was the Grail.

The Grail

The Grail turns up in different guises. One theory says the Grail is a metaphor for Jesus's bloodline – that he (in spite of the fact that we know next to nothing of the historical Jesus) had married Mary Magdalene. The descendants of this union then turn out to be an ancient royal French dynasty. In Celtic myth, as a symbol of transformation and renewal, the Grail relates to the Cauldron of Abundance; everywhere we find the theme of the spiritual, the mystical, the power to transform. In short, the Grail has the force of hidden mystery, the occult. When the texts speak of its 'life-giving' qualities, it is certainly meant in a religious sense – but with one proviso, for the true sense of the word 're-ligion' means to 'reconnect', to rediscover the spiritual source of our true Self, to become whole. Yet the majority of the medieval Grail romances are not explicit about the powers of the Grail (with one notable exception, as we shall see).

The *Perlesvaus,* from around 1191, does at least contain some teasing hints about the Grail's significance, and is so richly symbolic that the story is worth telling more or less in full.

One of Arthur's squires, Chaus, has a potent dream the day before the king is due to enter the forest and pray. Chaus dreams of a chapel in the forest where the body of a knight lies, dressed in fine clothes and surrounded by flaming candles. The squire decides to steal one of the candles, but a huge black ogre demands that he return it, violently striking him. At that point Chaus wakes up to find that he has, in fact, been stabbed.

Nevertheless, he is able to warn the king before he dies. With this knowledge, Arthur sets out on his journey.

The king arrives at the chapel of St Austin, where he sees three people performing Mass: a priest, a virgin, and her son. Here he also learns, from a local hermit, of the calamity brought upon the land by the question the young Parzival failed to ask: 'Whom does the Grail serve?' Before his return home, Arthur hears a voice announce that the land will soon be redeemed and that he should gather his knights together to search for the Grail. During this court assembly, however, three mysterious women enter. The first is bald and appears riding on a white mule. The second also rides and carries a dog and a jewelled shield emblazoned with a red cross that had belonged to Joseph of Arimathea. The third is on foot, carries a whip and is driving white mules; with her other hand she fondles the star hanging round her neck.

Here the anonymous author has combined elements of Celtic myth, Christian tradition and the Greek theme of the threefold goddess. The bald woman symbolises innocence, purity, even virginity; the woman carrying the dog brings to mind the three-headed Greek Hecate with her hounds of Hades; the woman driving the mules is reminiscent of the Tarot card The Charioteer (though we are accustomed to a male figure here, at least one early deck – the Bembo – depicts a regal woman holding an orb being pulled by two white horses). The first woman tells Arthur about some of the evils that have occurred in his kingdom, mentioning a mysterious cart, drawn by three white harts, standing outside the castle. Inside the cart lie 150 heads, sealed in gold, silver and lead. These metals represent the three stages of transformation in alchemy (covered in the next chapter). Their inclusion indicates that we are being presented with a coded mystery: for what might a Celto-Christian legend recounting the exploits of chivalrous knights have to do with a pseudo-science like alchemy?

The *Perlesvaus* continues with the failed attempts of Gawain and Lancelot to win the Grail. Gawain, though accompanied by the talismanic sword that had beheaded John the Baptist, forgets to ask the necessary question. Lancelot, because of his fatal love for Guinevere, Arthur's wife, is condemned from the outset to fail. All hopes are then invested in Parzival (here called Perceval) to recover the Grail. He discovers that the king of Castle Mortal has murdered his uncle, the Fisher King, and now lives in the Grail castle. Here Perceval is the 'good knight', attempting to avenge the death of his uncle, though in a later anonymous version, *La Folie Perceval,* the knight is the eponymous fool: young, naive and still to be initiated into the mysteries of life.

During his adventures Perceval meets a mysterious wise woman and, later, two lovers sitting beneath a tree who ask him to retrieve a golden apple possessed by a giant. We also meet the Four Grail Hallows again; the procession inside the castle consists of the chalice-bearing maiden, a page with the lance that pierced the side of Jesus; and four servants carrying a box and bearing a sword. Inside the box, however, is the 'book of the holy vessel' lying on a sacred platter, which Perceval cannot bear to look at because it 'shone with so great a light'. Here then, uniquely, the Grail is synonymous with a holy 'book' of wisdom, and Perceval is the fool who has yet to uncover the meaning of his own destiny.

Returning to the *Perlesvaus*, Perceval finally succeeds in becoming the new Grail king. For a time he lives in the forest, waiting for the ship that will take him towards the Blessed Isles. From this time onwards, it is said, no one else has seen the Grail.

We shall look at Wolfram's magical conception of the Grail in the next chapter. It makes more explicit the kind of hidden mysteries hinted at in the *Perlesvaus* and the *Folie*, where the Holy Grail is revealed as a 'book'. What follows now is an exploration of the Celtic concept of the Otherworld, one of whose names is the Blessed Isles, Perceval's ultimate destination.

## The Otherworld: a warning

Voyages undertaken to reach the Celtic Otherworld are rife in early Irish texts; it is a paradise, a place of perfection, often accessible only by a dangerous bridge. Other synonyms in the texts are the Fortunate Island, the Honeyed Plain of Bliss and the Island of Apples. It is not quite heaven, however, but a place where life proceeds in much the same way as in the earthly realm, except there is no suffering and none of the usual limitations of time and space. Heroic feats are everyday occurrences and learning and wisdom abound. The Irish god Manannan explains, for instance, that the Well of Segais, with its 'shining fountain' of five streams, represents 'the five senses through which knowledge is obtained. And no one will have knowledge who drinks not a draught out of [it].'

The physical locations of these Blessed Otherworlds were originally seen as occupying the same physical plane as Britain, and were found by sailing in a westerly direction. So, for example, Manannan's chief location, 'Emain Abhlach', is the Isle of Arran (off the west coast of Scotland), identified by some as Avalon. The Otherworld, as we might expect, enjoys perfect weather too: in Tennyson's *Idylls of the King* Arthur declares he is 'going a long way ... to the island-valley of Avilion; where falls not hail or rain or any snow, nor ever wind blows loudly'.

If it is not heaven, nor an underworld hell full of foreboding and human torment, it can be viewed as a kind of paradise on earth. In another variant on the Arthurian cycle, following his defeat at the battle of Camlan, the king is taken to a place where crops are richly abundant and 'apple trees spring up from the short grass in its woods' – the Island of Apples. We have met this symbol in the story of Perceval; in *La Folie Perceval,* he meets the lovers, and apples are a common motif in myth, in particular for their association with immortality. In classical mythology, Zeus is given the Golden Apples of the Hesperides; an immortal dragon guarded them. The source for such stories seems clear: the Tree of the Knowledge of Good and Evil is identified with the Tree of Life God placed in Eden, recounted in Genesis. We know that Eve tasted its tempting fruit despite God's prohibition. Just as the appearance of the serpent anticipates the expulsion of Adam and Eve from the Garden, the Celtic Otherworld, despite outward appearances, contains something truly rotten.

From the modern standpoint the Otherworld is an archetypal image of the perfect reality. It is a 'place' where we have probably all been at some time, and in the magical context it is an attitude of mind that must be brought under the control of the will if the magic is to succeed. In the Celtic conception the Otherworld exists as a reminder of the magic that converges with everyday reality; the trick is not getting lost in the former as we foolishly avoid the latter. You do not need to be a magician to feel the pull and enchantment of glamour; it takes you 'out of yourself' and into another realm. The mistake is often trying to hold on to it, to 'earth' the beautiful vision and try to recreate the glory of the Otherworld in this world. Something similar happens when we fall head over heels in love (though no one experiencing this state of ecstasy wants to be told that the rapture will not last for ever).

The Otherworld is a place of dreams come true where we shall want for nothing, as Adam and Eve found before the Fall. Eden is the Judaeo-Christian Paradise (the word means 'enclosed garden'), the walled space where we are protected, the state of womb-like Unconciousness before we incarnate into the world. The womb-Eden metaphor is not a mere play on words: the longing to return to this state of ideal perfection manifests itself in the person who habitually avoids 'real life', or who sacrifices his or her individuality to some impossible ideal, or who is narcissistically committed to 'staying young and beautiful' well into middle age, or worse, beyond it.

In all these cases something is being avoided: the real world where people make bad choices, suffer and grow old. The theme of immortality in the Otherworld is another symbol for the ageless Spirit (just as one might say 'you are only as old as you feel'), though quite often some kind of protective amulet is required to get there. For instance, the Celtic hero Bran, son of Febal, possesses a Silver Branch taken from an apple tree: this guarantees that he will remain ageless and ensures a safe return into the physical world, for the branch bears both divine and earthly characteristics. One day, however, a member of his company is stricken with feelings of homesickness; as they prepare to disembark they discover that countless years have passed, though they themselves have not aged. The homesick man, however, happily leaps on to dry land, only to be turned instantly to dust. He had presumably forgotten to pack his magical amulet, his Silver Branch whose roots lie in the mortal world, and which would have made his re-emergence into the plane of time and space successful.

Tintagel

This is what happens to many who return unwarily from the fantasy-laden, enchanted Otherworld: the real world facing them, with its tiresome obligations and frustrations, instantly turns their dreams to dust again. In psychology this is related to the motif of the *puer aeternus,* the Eternal Youth who will do anything to avoid becoming the Father, the symbol of worldly responsibility who has learned through time and effort how to *contain* the Otherworld. This is an important theme for those on the magical path. Any magical spell or invocation, or visualisation technique used to 'empower' the Unconscious, is an attempt to bring elements of the Otherworld into this world; in one's imagination, anything is possible. You should never place too high an expectation on your own efficacy here, however, especially if you have not followed the techniques properly. In other words, people may come to the magical altar expecting all kinds of miracles, and are disenchanted when their spells do not work quickly. (In some cases they do not work at all, often because of poor practice.) The marvellous Otherworld of instantly fulfilled dreams has to be seen for what it is, with its own laws and regulations. Or, if you prefer, magic only works by following the correct steps. This is what experienced magicians do every time they 'close' a spell and 'return' to the everyday world; they forget about the magic and allow the forces that exist to get on with their work. In other words, the magical and physical each require different attitudes, as the wise woman warns Bran before his journey: 'Let not your intoxication overcome thee.' In Celtic myth the Otherworld enchants us because it is so very like ours, a perfect place that can be reached just beyond the horizon. It can also be seen as a warning, however, to those who forget they live in this world, where things are rarely, if ever, perfect.

# Chapter 5
# The Magical Vessel

*'You say you yearn for the Grail. You foolish man,*
*I am grieved to hear that.*
*For no man can ever win the Grail unless*
*he is known in heaven ...'*

Wolfram von Eschenbach, *Parzival*

I n the year 1118 a nobleman, Hugues de Payen, went to the palace of Badouin, the king of Jerusalem. He was accompanied by eight other men and they offered the king their loyal service to keep the roads and highways safe and protect pilgrims on their way to the Holy Land. The king was delighted and installed the nine men in a part of his palace which, it is said, stood on the site of the ancient Temple of Solomon. The men had taken a vow of poverty and so the Order of the Poor Knights of Christ and the Temple of Solomon was established.

These nine men worked for the next nine years, guarding the roads to the Holy Land. As the Order expanded to become the Knights Templar, they became renowned for their strict obedience to Christian virtues, symbolised by their pure white mantles, which in time would also bear a red cross. Their military prowess was remarkable, as was their dedication to their role as the 'militia of Christ' on the battlefield, for no quarter was asked and each Templar had to fight to the death whatever the situation. Answerable only to the Pope himself, they became a mighty, independent force across continental Europe, amassing stupendous wealth as noble families whose sons had been admitted to the Order provided donations of money and property.

As their strength and fame increased, nobles and monarchs around the world sought their advice on matters of state; others were envious and voiced their resentment. In 1252, Henry III of England, for example, disapproved of their 'liberties and charters' and their 'enormous possessions', which made them feverish with 'pride and haughtiness'. The king threatened to confiscate some of their lands, to which the Templar Master retorted that to do so would be an unjust violation of his powers: 'So long as thou dost exercise justice thou wilt reign. But if thou infringe it, thou wilt cease to be king.' Perhaps it was this very arrogance, the presumption that the Knights Templar possessed the means even to unmake kings, that spelled the beginning of their end. By 1307 Philippe IV of France had had them arrested, and seven years later the last Grand Master of the Temple was slowly burned alive, issuing a curse on Philippe as his body was given over to the flames.

The arrest and imprisonment of the Knights was accompanied by the seizure of their property. The Inquisition, which had raided their preceptory (teaching institute) in the French capital, recorded that, among the seized goods, was a reliquary, 'a great head of gilded silver, most beautiful and constituting the image of a woman. Inside were two headbones, wrapped in a cloth of white linen, and another red cloth around it. A label was attached, on which was written the legend CAPUT LVIIIm ['Head 58m']. The bones inside were those of a rather small woman.' By the following year the Inquisition had compiled a list of formal charges relating to the Templars' supposed worship of a bearded male head: item 46 states that this idol was of a man's skull with three faces.

We will return to these incriminations shortly, but if we consider the female skull and bones we also find them in a legend of unknown provenance identified with the Templars' silver reliquary. Here, a woman who had died young was visited by her lover as she lay fresh in the grave. The lover exhumed her body and made love to 'her'. Then an eerie voice sounded instructing him to return after nine months, for then a son would be born to him. When he returned at the stated time, however, he found only a skull and two leg bones arranged like a cross. The voice returned, telling him to 'guard it well, for it would be the giver of all good things'. Thus the lover was able to vanquish any opponents because of the powers bestowed on this magical head.

As for the male idol the Templar Knights were accused of worshipping, the Inquisition records, with no apparent sense of bewilderment, that 'they said that the head could save them ... that [it could] make riches ... that it made trees flower ... that it made the land germinate'.

No doubt you will already have noticed the allusions here to the 'magical vessel' of Celtic tradition; it is irrelevant whether the Knights Templar actually made this head a figure of veneration, or whether we are looking at trumped-up charges by the Inquisition. I shall look at some of these mysteries at the end of this chapter, for they relate to Wolfram's version of the Holy Grail; what concerns us now is the significance of the Celtic 'magic' head:

## The cult of the vessel

*'And one day, towards the end of the year, as Caridwen was culling plants and making incantations, it chanced that three drops of the magic liquor flew out of the cauldron and fell upon the finger of Gwion Bach. And because they were very hot, he put his finger to his mouth, and the instant he put those marvel-working drops into his mouth, he foresaw everything that was to come ...'*

From the *Mabinogion*

The 'Caridwen' here is Cerridwen, the Celtic sorceress 'skilled in the magic arts' who boils a cauldron of inspiration and knowledge which, after a year and a day, will produce three blessed drops of the grace of inspiration. It is these that the youthful Gwion Bach, who has been told to guard the cauldron, accidentally tastes. His newly gained insight into the future, however, reveals that Cerridwen might turn her magical powers on him – and so he flees. He must, of course, pay for this and Cerridwen is finally avenged when, in the form of a 'high crested black hen', she finds Gwion in the guise of a grain of corn. He is swallowed by the dark goddess, who bears the grain for nine months and eventually gives birth to the beautiful and gifted Taliesin, who is to become the greatest of the Welsh poets.

Whatever else this tale may symbolise, I feel it says much about the process of initiation into Life. So often it is a goddess figure who presides over the ultimate attainment of wisdom, just as the Lady of the Lake's demand of Arthur prefigures the quest for the Grail. We have met this aspect of fate in Celtic myth in the Morrighan and the dark powers of the Feminine mystery, but the unfortunate Gwion Bach is not ready for it. His tasting of the three drops of inspiration is not intentional: it is an accident of Fate for which, despite his ability to foretell the future, he must suffer. The gift of insight is therefore both blessing and curse; yet, as his symbolic death approaches (Cerridwen as the black hen), and he is 'eaten' in the form of a grain of corn, he is ultimately transformed into the beautiful bard Taliesin.

Despite its obvious connotations with the seasonal cycles of decay and growth, the death and rebirth process is here, I feel, a psychological one. It is as if by his 'unfortunate' action of tasting the drops from the cauldron, Gwion Bach has himself engineered the whole process of transformation. This is how the Unconscious seems to work in everyday life, too, drawing us into situations that, however calamitous at first, result in greater consciousness. Of course, this new awareness does not appear overnight: following the sacrificial death and 'eating' of Gwion, the initial digesting of the experience, a nine-month period of gestation follows before the gifted Taliesin is born.

The symbol of the Cauldron – a receptacle in which the raw stuff of life is 'cooked' and so transformed – appears, too, in the story of the giant god-hero Bran. King of the Isle of the Mighty (Britain), Bran joined battle with the Irish king Matholwych, into whose hands the Magic Cauldron had fallen. Matholwych's men were able to resurrect their dead soldiers by the grace of the Cauldron, a detail we have met with on the Gundestrup Bowl:

*'Then the Irish kindled a fire under the cauldron of renovation, and they cast the dead bodies into the cauldron until it was full, and the next day they came forth fighting-men as good as before, except that they were not able to speak.'*

However, the decapitated head of Bran certainly could. When the battle is lost, and Bran is fatally injured in the foot with a poisoned dart, he makes the ultimate sacrifice, telling his men that they should cut off his head:

*'And take you my head and bear it even unto the White Mount
in London, and bury it there, with the face towards France ...
And a long time will you be upon the road ... And all that
time the head will be to you as pleasant company as it ever
was when on my body ... So they cut off his head, and these
seven went forward therewith.'*

The Head of Bran will speak to these seven men with
prophecies and has qualities reminiscent of the Otherworld.
During a long journey carrying it to a magical hall (where they
live for 80 years), they remember nothing of their previous lives
with its miseries and regrets, 'unconscious of having ever spent
a time more joyous and mirthful'. It is only when they open a
forbidden door that they suddenly remember again all the evils
of the world. There are obvious echoes here of Eden, with its
sealed-in state of bliss, whose marvellous spell is broken by
human curiosity. The Cauldron of Renewal, Bran's head and
the magical hall repeat this idea of an object or place, in
particular a mystical, interior space, that can bestow the gift of
immortality. Bran tells his men, 'a long time will you be on the
road', an allusion to the long road of life itself.

Before exploring more of this magical head, let us look
briefly at another Celtic decapitation theme with the tale of
Gawain and the Green Knight. One Christmas at the court of
Arthur, a hideous green-skinned figure in green clothes bursts
in on the assembly and suggests a dare for any knight with

sufficient mettle. The Green Knight will suffer a blow from his own axe on condition that he returns it a year later to the man who will undertake this task. At this, Gawain steps up and severs the man's head from his body. The Green Knight simply replaces the head upon his shoulders, telling Gawain they have a rendezvous in a year's time at the Green Chapel, when it will be the Green Knight's turn to strike the blow.

During the year, as Gawain looks for the Green Chapel, he meets Sir Bercilak who, while out hunting, says he knows where it is situated. Bercilak's wife gives Gawain a magical green baldric, which makes the wearer impervious to harm. Gawain finds the chapel where the Green Knight is waiting for him. Wearing his protective sash, Gawain reluctantly offers his head to be severed; at the third blow, the hideous Green Knight merely nicks him on the neck. Unexpectedly, the Green Knight then declares that the 'game' is over and reveals his true identity as Sir Bercilak.

Symbolically, these figures all embody aspects of the same principle. Novelist Lindsay Clarke suggests that an enforced severing of the head symbolises the 'removal' of the clever, conscious intellect with its pat, superficial answers to life. We can then begin to use the heart, to feel, to allow the powers of the intuitive realm to work, just as, paradoxically, Bran's head becomes 'magical' only when removed. I feel there is some merit in this, but it is not merely the willingness to 'remove one's head', to transcend the logical, everyday world that leads

The Green Man

to a more integrated view of life; it is important to any magical 'apprenticeship', too.

The theme of 'greenery' is also rife in the story. This is a symbol for anyone aspiring to magic. Green symbolises the naive hero, like Parzival, the aspirant on the path, not yet initiated. Green symbolises a state of 'unripeness', like unripe fruit in the natural world. In the same way, in the Border ballad *Thomas the Rhymer* the eponymous apprentice wears 'a coat of the elven cloth, and a pair of shoes of velvet green'. The Green Man decapitation theme of Celtic myth is also buried deep within a much later legend, the Little Gest of Robin Hood. Strands of magical tradition lie in the episode where Little John, injured and unwilling to let his enemies capture him alive, entreats Robin:

> *'Better to take your noble sword*
> *And smite clean off my head:*
> *Give me wounds both deep and wide –*
> *But make sure I am dead.'*

Though the more familiar image of Robin of the Greenwood has obscured his roots as a kind of Celtic Pan or Silvanus, the mischievous woodland spirit of classical myth, the etymological source of the name betrays these roots. 'Robin' is a later form of *hob*, meaning a sprite or elf, from which is derived 'hobgoblin'; 'Hood' has shadowy origins in the old English *hod*, related to *heafod* or the suffix *haedu* – the head. The latter may mean nothing more than that Robin Hood is so called because he is the 'head' of a gang of outlaws; on the other hand, it can also be seen to underline the connection between the fertility of nature and the magical Celtic head. The celebration of the fruits of the earth in the Celtic Feast of Lughnasadh is identified with another mythic figure from the ancient folk air 'John Barleycorn Must Die'. Nigel Pennick comments that the song is 'the explicit description of the mystery of death and rebirth that underlies the ethos of Northern Tradition shamanism and magic'.

John Barleycorn is the spirit of the fields who is at first declared dead; at springtime, however, he 'got up again and sore surprised them all', and by summer has grown a long beard. By autumn, however, he has, 'sicken'd more and more [and] faded into age', at which point he is dismembered, his bones crushed in a mill and his blood drunk. Yet the victory is all his, for in John Barleycorn's second incarnation as bread and ale, there is joy and feasting as everyone toasts his name.

There are elements here of the shaggy Green Man and the sick king (not to mention the Christian communion), but I feel the Green Man figure is not merely a symbol of pagan fertility, the 'greenery' of leaves and vines and fecund nature, but is concerned with a much deeper level: the creative process itself, the mysterious forces that lead to growth, the 'miracle' inherent in the fact of nature's renewal and rebirth. Thus figures like the goatish Robin Goodfellow (another early form of Robin

Hood), heavily bearded, cloven-hoofed and with an erect phallus, is at once about sexual fertility and the more spiritual promise of regeneration and immortality. The penis represents the life-creating energies within the psyche. Just as the Fisher King injured in the groin is a symbol of spiritual 'illness', so the forces for change, growth and awareness begin with the severed head of the Green Man. Caesar tells us that the Celts believed that the head contained the soul. It is therefore the repository of divine wisdom, with the power to work miracles, as with the alleged Templar head. If we add the Magic Cauldrons of the Daghda and Cerridwen and the mystical Grail, we have three related symbols – Cauldron, Head, Grail – that combine the theme of a magical transmutation.

## The Grail and the Stone

*'Flegetanis the heathen saw with his own eyes in the constellations the things he was shy to talk about, hidden mysteries. He said there was a thing called the Grail, whose name he had read clearly in the constellations. A host of angels had left it there.'*

Wolfram von Eschenbach, *Parzival*

In Wolfram's version of the Grail quest, he tells us about the wonders this much sought-after object possesses. It is 'the fruit of blessedness', able to provide the person of noble aspiration with 'whatsoever one reached out one's hand for'. It contains 'such abundance, the sweetness of the world, that its delights were very like what we are told of the kingdom of heaven', and it may also come as no surprise that the Order of knights who guard the sanctuary of the Grail in Wolfram is called 'Templeisen'. Despite the insistence of some authors that this must refer to the historical Knights Templar, no such identification is necessary. We have already seen how the exploits of the Templars are the stuff of legend, and how the miraculous head they are said to worship is reminiscent of Celtic lore. Those investigating the history of the Templars are also perplexed by the idea of just nine knights being able to protect the roads leading to the Holy Land, and that they admitted no new members into the Order for another nine years. History is mute regarding the early deeds of the Templars. Moreover, there is no evidence of them doing anything to protect pilgrims. This is why some authors have seen the power of metaphor at work, especially in the symbolic number nine.

Nine, representing a magical cycle of completion (as with the birth of Taliesin) or full initiation, is a common mythic theme. According to Jolande Jacobi it 'has been a "magic number" for centuries ... it represented the perfected form of the perfected Trinity in its Threefold elevation'. In Celtic myth there are Nine Sisters presiding over the otherworldly Island of Apples; this is echoed in the Nine Muses of classical legend and Egypt's Nine Gods at Anu. Nine is associated with the means towards spiritual perfection; in modern terms, with the whole, integrated psyche that has understood itself and finally come to terms with life in all its varied forms. So the nine Knights Templar who 'guard the way for pilgrims' and preside over the mysteries of the Grail evoke the same ideas we have seen with Arthur's Grail Knights. Though set in a historical context, the story of the Templars is another form of sacred story-telling, where the 'dangerous route' to the 'Holy Land' is the spiritual path of all – and not an easy one to take.

The real point is that Wolfram reminds us he is concealing an important mystery, one hidden in the Grail, for 'however wise a man may be, he will surely be glad to know what are the guiding thoughts in this narrative'. Wolfram declares he obtained his knowledge of the Grail from Kyot de Provence, who learned about it from the heathen Flegetanis mentioned in the quote on page 102. Wolfram says that these enigmatic figures were reluctant to divulge the 'hidden mysteries' of the Grail, and that the Grail Knights 'are nourished by a stone of most noble nature ... it is called *lapsit exillis*' for, in a departure from other medieval romances, 'the stone is also called the Grail'. This mysterious stone has the power to confer immortality, for it arrived from heaven. The obscure Latin term *lapsit exillis* has been identified with *lapis ex celis* (the 'stone from heaven') or *lapis exilis* (the 'exiled stone'). Both readings are relevant to our study of the Grail-as-stone. In the first case the stone from heaven is identified as the emerald that fell from

Lucifer's crown as he was cast out of heaven. In the second, it is the rejected 'corner stone' of both alchemical and Christian tradition; in fact, the lapis elixir is the much-sought Philosopher's Stone.

Wolfram has therefore used the foundation of an essentially Celtic motif and identified it with one just as perplexing from the alchemist's laboratory. The Stone's relevance to magic cannot be understated, and there are as many extravagant claims made for the powers of the Grail as there are for the Philosopher's Stone. In the view of modern psychology, the Grail/Stone is synonymous with the Self and its other related mythic symbols such as Treasure, Mandala, or anything made of gold. From this point of view it is what we are all unconsciously seeking: as the psyche instinctively unfolds towards greater awareness, so the individual slowly comes to embody the unique Self that was always present.

Though such consciousness is not won without a price, the Grail/Stone represents the individual's quest for some kind of spiritual meaning: it is a return journey for each individual, towards self-knowledge. However, this is a deeper knowledge not merely about our innermost selves, our most profound sense of the religious or spiritual, but about the secret workings of matter, too: the realisation that some secret part of the individual has meaningfully fashioned the events in his or her life. Whether we call this the Unconscious or the Universal Mind is neither here nor there; what it is important to realise is that the gradual unfolding of fate, destiny, the power of the Grail, may not after all be meaningless, blind chance. In short, there may be a point at which one realises that everything 'fits' and coalesces into a coherent whole.

The alchemists also searched for the secrets of matter, the workings of the material world, how and why events manifested in their lives as they did, and they were in no doubt that the source was the divine spark within: that secret Self, the blessed Philosopher's Stone. In a rare candid moment, Morienus declares: 'This thing is extracted from you; you are its mineral ... if you recognise this the love and approbation of the stone will grow within you.'

Though many alchemists' texts are full of mystifying words and images, other Philosophers were prepared to be less obscure. As Gerhard Dorn says:

*There is in natural things a certain truth which cannot be seen with the outward eye ... and of this the Philosophers have had experience, and have ascertained that its virtue is such as to work miracles ... As faith works miracles in man, so this power, the* veritas efficaciae, *brings them about in matter. This truth is the highest power and an impregnable fortress wherein the stone of the philosophers lies hid.'*

Despite the high-sounding claims, this is just another way of expressing the occult aphorism 'like attracts like', though this truth must first be sought and wrested from its 'impregnable fortress'. Dorn's 'efficacious truth' is the absolute faith one must have in one's goal before undertaking any magical work, identified here as the 'highest power' contained in the Stone. The need for belief without reservation is expressed in this way in the anonymous Golden Tract: 'if you know the beginning, the end will duly follow by the help of God'.

To the pre-scientific mind, powers such as those suggested by the miracle-working Stone were to be marvelled at, hence Wolfram's rather florid language when describing the Grail. Such powers were also not to be divulged easily, hence the emphasis on secrecy and outwardly beguiling allegory, accessible only to other practitioners. So we may regard the Grail/Stone as an item of 'magical power' (faith) or as a symbol of one's spiritual destiny (wisdom and self-understanding); there is really no ultimate difference between the two. The former often begets the latter, but both relate to the miracle of nature. The secret workings of matter (or energy) are still as much a mystery to the modern physicist or magician as they were to the old Philosophers.

What we can say is that what we do to the world, it does back to us. Quite why, we do not know. An individual's very thoughts create his or her own larger world; to paraphrase the poet Novalis, Soul and Fate are two names for the same principle (but the principle is the real mystery). The alchemist saw us bound up in the great experiment that is life, a great work that is the attempt to discover our own Stone, but which can be revealed only by the effort to burn away the ignorance concealing it. This may take a whole lifetime, but whatever form one's life takes, we are all changed by it.

For the first-time seeker, this initial contact with the Self is often felt as a profound inner revelation. In a significant coda to the *Perlesvaus,* two knights visit the Grail Castle many years after Perceval's exploits. The castle is now dilapidated and ghosts are rumoured to haunt it occasionally. Nevertheless, the two knights spend some time there and return somehow 'different'. To those who ask, they will reveal nothing of what happened to them, offering only the enigmatic reply: 'Go there and you will see what we have seen.'

# Chapter 6
# The Celtic Legacy

It is said that the River Boyne in Ireland flowed from a sacred pool that appeared out of the earth, in a grove surrounded by nine wise hazel trees. Their fruit, the hazel nuts, would sometimes fall into the water, imbuing the pool with divine wisdom; so too, the River Boyne, for salmon carried the wisdom upstream. One day, an apprentice called Finn McCool was with a wise teacher who had finally caught the Salmon of Knowledge, from which one could gain all the gnosis (knowledge of spiritual mysteries) in the universe. As the fish cooked over a fire and the teacher prepared for contemplation, he told Finn to oversee the cooking, warning him not to taste the Salmon. As the fish's skin blistered,

however, the apprentice pressed down with his thumb and burned himself. He put his thumb in his mouth to soothe the pain and at once acquired all the mysterious wisdom of the world.

Although we have met something similar in the story of Gwion Bach, this legend is typical of Celtic themes, where water is seen as a source of divine knowledge. Archaeology abounds with examples of votive offerings: animal bones, wooden carvings or military hardware, found in Irish and Welsh lakes and rivers, including the Severn, the Thames and the Seine. Certain rivers even derive their names from a particular goddess: there is the Danube for Dana (or Don) and the rivers Brent and Braint for Brigantia (Brighid). These water offerings are not simply a matter of wanting to appease a deity, however; rivers, pools and streams were considered entrances to the Otherworld, the place from which the elusive mysteries of life flow in and out of the 'real' world. Hence, certain sacred rivers are, like the magical Salmon, 'carriers' of wisdom; sacrificing one's material possessions as votive offerings is a way of reaching closer to the source of life. Thus, giving up one's highly valued material treasures is essentially a magical act based on the law of exchange: 'as ye give, so shall ye receive'.

It is clear from the story of Finn McCool that the receipt of divine knowledge was the greatest treasure one could hope to gain. However, in Celtic myth the mysteries of water itself speak of something even more sublime: water is a symbol of the way life is. In other words, water, as a symbol of both the Goddess and life in general, is fluid, changeable, the place where one thing flows imperceptibly into another. This idea of 'liquid' energy as the root of all reality is found in modern physics, and of Celtic religion Anne Bancroft writes:

*'The whole world was interlinked and interrelated ... [taking] its form as shifting, or metamorphosis ... The material form was never rigid and autonomous, as we see it today, never merely a "thing", or self created, but always liquid, dancing, filled with the otherness of the spirit.'*

What we would now call ancient superstitions have survived in various forms since the dawn of the Celts. One water rite, in particular, used to be performed in the Outer Hebrides until the late nineteenth century. The islanders of Lewis, in a ceremony presided over by a pagan priest (rather like a scene from *The Wicker Man*) would offer up a libation of ale to the water god Shony. The priest, standing waist deep in the sea and lifting the cup above his head, offered hope for 'plenty of sea-war [seaweed] for enriching our ground for the ensuing year'. The ceremony would be performed on 31 October, when the ancient dark goddess Cailleach (a counterpart of the Morrighan) would stalk the land. This date is, of course, familiar to everyone as Hallowe'en, but it is also the start of the Celtic calendar, which essentially plots the cycle of growth in nature and whose echoes are seen in the many folk customs it has spawned.

The Glamis Stone

## The Celtic year

The Celtic year is divided into eight parts, though its real significance is derived from its four major 'fire festivals', celebrated on a full moon closest to the date in question. We are accustomed to marking out the progress of the solar year with the two solstices of summer and winter (21 June and 21 December) and the equinoxes of spring and autumn (21 March and 21 September). The latter marks the onset of gathering blackness, when nights are longer than the days and it is clear that the land will admit no new growth.

The Celtic New Year begins in darkness on 1 November; as Christianity grew in influence 31 October became known as All Saints' Eve and 1 November as All Hallows Day, to drive out the malign spirits that were said to be at large (hence the superstition regarding evil witches, a Christian development). Originally it was called Samhain, a festival connected with the slaughter of excess cattle that could not be kept alive through the winter. The parts of the carcasses not eaten would then be ritually burned, hence 'bonfire' and its origin in 'bone-fire'. However, in its connection with Cailleach, the Dark Annis, or the Grey or Blue Hag, it is a period of darkness and mystery, divination, prophecy, and commemoration of the ancestral dead. Significantly, it is the time of year when the fiery Celtic warrior Cuchulainn met his death; a time when the solar-based ego must relinquish power. For here we are in the realm of the Goddess and fate, and since it is neither quite the end of autumn nor the start of winter, it is an uncertain 'grey area' between the worlds of light and dark, as Shirley Toulson eloquently puts it:

*'The two worlds come together in that awareness of the spiritual beings, whom we may sense but cannot see ... and whose silence is of the same nature as the silence of God; more alive than much of our restless chatter.'*

Thus we have a calendar that begins with the Feminine; indeed, the whole cycle relates to an essentially feminine phenomenon: the care and protection of the land.

Interestingly, there is also a powerful Celtic tale regarding the winter solstice. At Newgrange in County Meath is a stone sepulchre, consisting of a large mound with an inner chamber reached by a narrow passage. It is constructed so that the rays of the sun at dawn on the winter solstice shoot at once into the inner chamber. This was later interpreted as the fertile Daghda mating with one of his consorts: the Good God desired to make love to Boand, wife of Elcmar, who had been sent away and placed under a spell so he would not be aware of the passing of time. Elcmar was away for nine months but returned believing it was the same evening he had embarked on his journey. Daghda mated with Boand, and Oengus, the 'son who is conceived at dawn and born before dusk', was born. Though we are not fundamentally concerned with the significance of the solstices, this tale evokes the Celtic motif of the pre-eminent Feminine darkness, which nevertheless contains Daghda's 'seed' of light.

However, Cailleach/Boand must in turn give way to the bright goddess Brighid who presides over Oimelc (or Imbolc) on 1 February, and the Christian Candlemas on 2 February, when there is the first stirring of the Daghda's power in the earth and the first hint of approaching spring and the powers of light. For the Celts this fragile state of cosmic affairs was expressed in the birth of lambs, after which the ewes would come into milk. Lambs born then will feed on the abundant spring grass and be fat enough for market later on; it may have

Brighid

seemed miraculous that so many survived the cold. So Brighid is the maiden of the pasture; she later appears in Christian myth as Bride, whose cows gave milk three times a day and who could make food multiply at the very touch of her hand. Another tale relates how she caused a miracle to happen in Conwy during a fish famine: she threw a batch of rushes into the local stream and after a few days they had turned into fish.

Similar Christian legends tend to be rather two-dimensional, and usually exist as allusions to Christ's New Testament miracles and evidence of his continuing presence. More instructive is the tale of an old board game played in Rome at Oimelc. On one end of the board is the figure of a hag; at the other end sits a young woman. The hag sets a dragon loose to devour a lamb the young woman has released, though the lamb is, in fact, the victor. So the reign of Cailleach the hag ends at Oimelc, as she is overcome by the youthful Brighid. It is a state of innocence, when purifying cold winds pierce the air and the earth is ready to begin a new cycle. The Celts were thought to sacrifice cockerels at Oimelc; this may have been a ritual means of increasing the sun's power and hastening its return. Since cockerels noisily announce the sun's arrival every day at dawn, they are associated with rebirth and spiritual resurrection, so this practice combines the spiritual and the practical in fine Celtic style.

Daghda's seed begins to show fuller results during the festival of Beltane on 30 April; it was the real beginning of summer, when livestock were driven out into the open fields to graze. In a Druidic ceremony, the cattle were ritually herded between two massive bonfires as a protection against disease. Beltane (which some commentators interpret as 'goodly fire') is a period of growth and abundance, with flowers in bloom, birdsong and the forces of light prevailing. This is symbolised in the quaint legend of a Welsh monk, Brioc, who one day saw a pack of bloodthirsty wolves approaching. Though his companions fled at once, the hero Brioc sat in his chariot and the wolves were instantly calmed by his presence. In the same way, this sense of thanksgiving that the forces of the night have finally been tamed (or better still, integrated) survives in an old Gaelic blessing:

*'Everything within my dwelling or in my possession*
*All kine and crops, all flocks and corn,*
*From Hallow Eve to Beltane Eve.'*

'Beltane Eve' is, of course, the day before the more familiar May Day, with its celebratory garlands, milkmaids, morris dancers and hobby horses. Jack-in-the-Green, whom we have met in his other incarnations as Robin Hood and the Celtic Green Man, is ceremonially executed, with those in attendance making a grab at his foliage for good luck. Similar in essence to the rites of the mummer's play, these modern examples of street theatre hark back to the Celtic theme of death and rebirth, shown in the sick Fisher King, the decapitated Bran, and the ailing Arthur. The hobby horse, its operator dancing through the crowd and ritually bumping his snapping 'head' into the women, has also excited a great deal of comment, being seen as a rather crude enactment of male fertility and sexual swagger. Yet the horse's appearance in Celtic myth is far subtler. It is a feminine symbol embodied in the goddess Epona (from where 'pony' is derived) and her Welsh version, Rhiannon, whose songs lull the listener into the Otherworld. In turn, these are reflections of a far more ancient mother goddess whose power is embodied in her totem, the horse, and whose echoes appear in the tale of an ancient Irish chieftain who was ritually wedded to a mare, a word with its root in the Old English mere, a body of water. At its root, the hobby horse ritual is about 'mating' with the female powers of the Unconscious, that is, succumbing to – and not forcibly grasping – its mysteries and profound depth.

Sex is a common mythical theme that symbolises the 'union' of masculine ego and feminine Unconscious, but as Beltane is primarily a festival of light, I shall now look at the familiar symbol of the garlanded maypole. Here is a more obviously phallic emblem – despite children dancing round it – and several still survive in English villages. Sometimes the maypole is a real tree felled for the occasion, connecting it with Celtic roots and their extensive tree lore. Yet despite its sexual element, it also sits perfectly within the Beltane festival of the powers of light, since the ritual dancing that circles the maypole is also a kind of sympathetic magic, symbolising the bright rays of the sun and their generative force. It is not possible to state that this is its true source, but the spokes-within-a-wheel motif is a common symbol for the sun, whether it be the Celtic Cross or talismanic symbols from Norse tradition such as the fire wheel or heavenly star. All are representations of the power of the god that, from a common centre, spirals outwards and everywhere for all time.

The last of the major Celtic fire festivals is the Lughnasadh, the assembly of Lugh, which occurs on 1 August, the symbolic gathering in of nature's bounty. Of course, it was also a very real gathering in. Barley and wheat were ripe for harvesting, and a little later blackberries were picked from hedgerows and apples and nuts from trees: all this must be done before the next Samhain. After the corn harvest the first loaf of bread is baked from the new crop, hence the celebration referred to in the Lughnasadh's Anglo-Saxon name, Lammas, or 'loaf mass'.

It was a time of gathering in another sense: the tribes came together so the young folk might meet a prospective partner. So-called trial marriages were instituted. Each partner promised to stay together for a year and a day; if the 'marriage' failed after that time they parted. The god Lugh is, as we have seen, a patron of many magical skills, so the Lughnasadh was also a time of competitive, skilled games where, presumably, the young males could demonstrate their physical prowess to potential brides.

Far from the festival being simply a time of male showmanship, the goddess of the land is again a shadowy presence. It is said that the feast was inaugurated by Lugh in honour of his foster mother Tailtiu, who died after thoroughly exhausting herself clearing the land in time for cultivation. This presumably is the source for the corn dolly ceremony, when the last of the cropped wheatstalks would be fashioned into a female figure; at ploughing time it would be ritually driven into the soil. The archetypal ancient goddess of the land, whom we have already encountered in various guises, is often called

Sovereignty, for it is she who is the real presiding power behind nature, and the land to which the Celtic king is married. Thus, when an ancient Irish king, Conn, received a vision of Lugh, he saw him installed on a throne with his consort, the goddess Sovereignty.

In a more modern sense the Celtic year can be seen as a metaphor representing the cycle of human ageing or growing awareness: as we emerge from the darkness of the womb (Samhain), we enter the stage of incipient curiosity and the first springs of consciousness as children (Oimelc), that 'virgin' state of being where everything is fresh, new, untried. Beltane represents the period of awareness, the sense of a more adult experience where our lives have developed according to the seeds we have sown. It is also a transitional phase: it is not too late to change one's life. With Lammas we have entered the fullness of middle age and it is time to gather in the fruits of experience: it is the autumn of one's years when ideally one has, like Lugh, mastered the skills of life. Finally, as with the dark interior of the womb, we must return to the darkness of the earth like the humble corn dolly.

A Corn Dolly

In Philip Carr-Gomm's *The Druid Way,* he broadly relates each of the four fire festivals to a particular human rite of passage: he names Samhain 'Parting and Dying'; Oimelc, 'Birthing and Naming'; Beltane, 'Loving and Mating'; and Lughnasadh, 'Marrying and Meeting'. With Beltane, Gomm brings out what I feel to be the true sense of this festival, that of union and merging, which is why I stress that the shenanigans of the hobby-horse man symbolically depict the king-hero's sacramental mating with the supreme mother goddess, Sovereignty. The Celtic year is thus a Feminine phenomenon, celebrating the world of nature and matter, the archetypal Mother. The fourfold system we use to calculate the solar cycle (vernal equinox to winter solstice) is thus complemented by festivities at other times which give a sense of feminine completeness and wholeness to the yearly round.

## Of hills and giants

The gigantic hill figures found in southern England have attracted a great deal of speculation from scholarly historians and those interested in the occult. Much interest has centred on two in particular: one is a horse figure we now call the White Horse of Uffington; the other is a male giant, the Long Man of Wilmington. Despite years of research, no one has come up with any definitive answers regarding their appearance, who made them, or what their true significance is. Much the same applies to the many earthworks and cromlechs (stone circles) that exist throughout Britain. My purpose here is not to 'solve' the mystery, but to look at how such man-made features may have originated, and whether they offer clues to our Celtic past.

I will begin with one of the better-known (though even more mysterious) hill features, Silbury Hill near Marlborough in Wiltshire. This is a man-made 'tump', as distinct from a 'tumulus', which is an ancient burial mound. The distinction is made because Silbury, at 130 feet high (39.6 m), with a flattened top with a diameter of 100 feet (30.4 m), was definitely not used for burial purposes. During an excavation there in 1968, archaeologists did not find evidence of a Neolithic burial chamber but instead discovered a little conical mound (a smaller tump), beneath which were ropes, arranged in a radial-like pattern. We have met with this spoked-wheel/ sun motif before in the symbolic maypole dance at Beltane, and though the discovery may mean little to historians, it is of symbolic importance within Celtic tradition: it represents the radiant sun god wedded to the land.

According to Philip Carr-Gomm, the Silbury dig 'suggests it was a hill built for the Lughnasadh celebrations ... a giant man-made harvest hill'. At the Newgrange barrow in Ireland, where Daghda mated with Boand, there are circular, maze-like, spiral patterns carved into the outer kerbstone which, as with much of Celtic non-representational art, seem simultaneously symbolic of the inner and the outer worlds. In other words, in their very simple, abstract way, such designs represent energies spiralling outwards from the centre (the mysterious source of Life); as they take on their circular shape, the wheel of life, they form the manifest world. There are many ways of expressing this symbolic idea; the circle, representing the cyclical nature of reality (human and cosmic) at whose centre is some enigmatic source of power (the Self, God), is an ancient motif. This spiral-like motif is also found on a tump in Lewes, Sussex, its path encircling the conical mound until it reaches the flat summit.

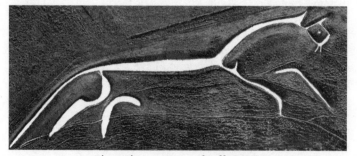

The White Horse of Uffington

The White Horse of Uffington in Berkshire is a spectacular 360 foot long (109.7 m) chalk figure, which appears to be leaping through the air towards the edge of a shallow ditch, an earth enclosure named Uffington Castle. (Just below the horse is a combe in the down where pagan-like cheese-rolling competitions once took place.) The horse's long neck and crude appearance have prompted some commentators to suggest that it might even be a dragon, though its similarity to horses on coins imported from Gaul and struck in early Britain is of note: both face left to right, and both have disjointed bodies and bird-like beaked heads. (Leaping horses and birds symbolise the flight of the soul after death.) The horse may be the work of a Celtic tribe of the first century BC; if so, it would commemorate the mother-goddess and her realm: nature itself.

The Long Man's counterpart is the Cerne Abbas Giant in Dorset, an 180 foot long (54.8 m) figure brandishing a club, whose erect phallus itself measures no less than 30 feet (9.1m). The sexual symbolism would seem self evident; indeed, tradition has it that couples would have sex there on May Day to ensure conception. Its association with paganism is also enhanced by the square enclosure above the giant's head, which was used for maypole celebrations.

The Long Man on Windover Hill, near Wilmington in Sussex, is an enigma. At 231 feet tall (70.4 m), a third taller than the Statue of Liberty, it is the largest such representation in the world. Standing with arms outstretched, and bearing no facial or other markings, he appears to be holding two long staves, one at each side of him. This has drawn the comment that if he was a solar god, he could be standing at the threshold of heaven, whose doors he has just opened. The mystery is in his posture: whereas the huge-shouldered Cerne Abbas Giant is full of bold aggression and sexual power, the Long Man stands

The Cerne Abbas Giant

calm and contemplative, clearly not a typical representation of rampant malehood. Compared with the straight, vertical trunk of the Cerne Abbas Giant, the curves of the Long Man – especially the hips and calves – are positively feminine. And there is something else one cannot fail to notice: the absence of a penis. Without drawing any dogmatic conclusions, the Long Man looks like a hermaphrodite, a kind of bisexual primal archetype – in the modern psychological sense a fusion or integration of male and female energies that form a whole being (the goal of alchemy). If this sounds too sophisticated for an ancient hill figure (or just plain far-fetched), Philip Carr-Gomm has studied the Long Man at close quarters and says there is quite clearly an indentation around the area of the Man's missing phallus: 'at the groin there is a depression in the earth like a vulva, at the chest there are two [depressed] breasts and the hips are clearly female, not male'.

Whether male or female, the gigantic figures that appear in the earth, foreshadow it in ancient legend or, like Bran and the Daghda, populate Celtic tradition, clearly belong to the realm of magic. In some cases they are the prime movers behind creation itself, as Dr Brian Bates' *Way of the Wyrd* has it:

*'The giants are the gods of old. The world was made from giants, in the first winter. A mighty giant was created from hoarfrost. And when the fire came, he melted. From the enormous bulk of his body came the worlds. From his blood flowed the sea, from his bones the mountains, from his hair the forests, from his skull the sky.'*

I believe that if there is any 'purpose' to these hill figures (apart from those in places that may have had a practical use, such as a burial chamber), it is in the fact of their very appearance. This may sound simplistic, but it must be remembered that in the Celtic world the goddess Sovereignty, with her mystery, power and unfathomable might, was everything to do with the land itself. The archetypal Celtic king was, of course, 'married' to her, and such man-made features are all too visible reminders of the deity's awe-inspiring power.

## Chapter 7
# Making Magic: Enhance Your Life

Celtic magic can take a variety of forms, from the alleged mystery rites of the Druids, to the commemorative fire festivals we looked at earlier and the pagan celebrations that survive today. There is also the great body of traditional stone and plant lore used in healing through the ages. We see much of this used in the practice of modern Wicca, with its emphasis on goddess archetypes and the natural cycles of life.

Yet a large part of Celtic tradition reveals a more intellectual side to the old teachings, first expressed orally and later transmitted in poetic form. This is especially true of the Irish and Welsh cycles; as we have seen, the power of eloquence, the binding power of the spoken word, was a kind of magical device in itself. The Gallic god of eloquence, Ogmius, was called Oghma in Ireland: he is grianainech, the 'sun-face', who is responsible for inventing what has since been termed the Celtic alphabet, Ogham.

## Ogham: the Celtic alphabet

This system of 20 characters is little more than a series of horizontal notches marked on either side of a median line, customarily carved in wood or stone.

B L F S   N H D T C   Q M G NG Z R   A O U E   I

### The Ogham Alphabet

Usually read from right to left or from bottom to top, at least 500 such markings can be seen on stone monuments in southern Ireland, for example. One concerns the story of the Fair Giantess, in which Finn McCool and his men, the Fianna, met the giant maiden Vivionn from the Land of Maidens (another synonym for the Otherworld). While the maiden was speaking a beautiful young man suddenly appeared. He threw his spear at Vivionn and the Fianna gave chase, but the maiden was mortally wounded. Finn buried her beneath a large mound on the spot where she died. He placed a stone pillar above and carved her name in Ogham.

Though Ogham's origins are unknown, scholars have seen connections with the ancient tree lore of the Celts, since each Ogham letter relates to a particular tree. This is a form of totemism, as each tree had its own magical or sacred property.

The oak occasionally produces the radiant Golden Bough; hazel is the traditional wood for making magical shields (its fruit, the hazel nut, is the 'fruit' of wisdom); birch is used to drive away evil and to make the maypole; rowan also protects against malign influence; and ash is the preferred wood for making a magician's wand.

The tradition of using a particular kind of wood in the construction of dwellings and household items also stems from this magical connection (as does the herbalist's use of tree bark to relieve ailments), for the specific tree would act as an amulet to protect against evil or mischievous spirits.

As we might expect, Ogham language had magical uses. According to the myth, Oghma said it should only be used in poetry by learned bards and wise men. In this sense it is a form of code, to be communicated among the initiated in verse form: various stressed words that began with a certain letter would invoke the totemic power (its essential 'spiritual' quality) of a corresponding tree. Thus, Caitlin Matthews says Ogham is:

*'... a Celtic method of inscription which has its roots in the treelore of native belief. When a word beginning with "b" was spoken it automatically resonated with the birch tree, with its lore, symbolism and power.'*

In the ancient Welsh poem *The Battle of the Trees,* the magician Gwydion (whose name comes from the same root as that of 'wisdom' and 'trees') names a mysterious man who 'unless his name were known could not be overcome'. In this obscure symbolic poem, which could be seen as a riddle to be solved, this enigmatic figure tells of his existence in different forms. It begins in the plural: 'Existing of yore ... from the time when the shout was heard, we were put forth, decomposed and simplified, by the tops of the birch,' but later is in the singular, 'frequent was the benefit of the Bard. I am he who influences the song of praise, which the tongue recites.'

This is just a tiny example of the poem's many archaic obscurities, yet the reference to birch as the primary tree or Ogham letter is clear enough, However, the 'he' in *The Battle of the Trees* would appear to be the power and eloquence of the spoken word itself, the eternal wisdom that is shaped into being by the poet. As Caitlin Matthews puts it: 'The real battle of the trees was one of words, of letters. The real warriors in this battle were the poets who wielded their oghams skilfully and to such effect.'

## The talisman: a magical device

In the light of this, let us look at how a wooden Celtic talisman was constructed. As a traditional magical 'device' for attracting good luck, the talisman is traditionally 'charged' to perform a specific task via an appropriate ritual, through the particular symbol it bears. Some sources say a properly prepared talisman possesses powers independent of the user, i.e. it will work whether or not you believe in it. David Conway says: 'the efficacy of a talisman does not depend entirely on the faith its owner places in it ... [but on its] intrinsic magic'. This seems to be somewhat of a reversal of the modern view, and even the Renaissance philosopher Paracelsus claimed that 'the exercise of true magic does not require any ceremonies or conjurations, or the making of circles and signs'.

In other words, 'true magic' is dependent on the powers unearthed by the magician; without these, Conway's 'intrinsic magic' cannot function as intended. In short, as with all magic, its efficacy is entirely dependent on the energies of the individual will. Moreover, this must combine with the Universal Will, or Universal Mind, the intelligent, ordering principle of Life that is at once universal and a property of the Unconscious. (Jung called this phenomenon the Self, a factor at work in the 'meaningful coincidences' of apparent fate.)

However, if a successful magical spell is first and foremost about actual possibilities, or what Ophiel calls the 'sphere of availability', the real 'trick' lies in conveying one's magical desires and objectives, as it were, to the Universal Mind. If this is done successfully it will certainly result in one's goal 'coming true'. This often entails a complete suspension of logic, a belief in belief itself, a wholehearted acceptance that such 'magical' forces can be invoked. The will is harnessed to belief, or as Paracelsus puts it: 'the will creates forces that have nothing to do with reason but obey blindly'. Of course, this is easier said than done, and one of the reasons for 'the making of circles and signs' is the symbolic power they release in the individual. Such symbols are able to 'work' on the Unconscious and so evoke a response in a way that ordinary language cannot.

## Make your own Celtic talisman

The instructions overleaf show you how to construct a general-purpose talisman within the tradition of Celtic lore. I call it 'Brighid's Wheel' (see Fig. 2) and it is based on the Celtic 'Finn's (McCool) Shield', which is an amulet or protective device. Whereas amulets are essentially a protection against negative energies, talismans work more or less the other way round, by encouraging positive energies.

Brighid's Wheel

Ideally the Wheel should be made of oak, the old symbolism stating that its fruit, the acorn, is a powerful token of potential. Not only was the oak sacred to the Druids, but it also appears in *The Battle of the Trees,* where 'the complete number of nine hundred pertained to me'. This is because oaks are said to live for 900 years, so the Spirit of the Bard is aligned with the power of the oak, as a symbol of stability, endurance and wisdom. Alternatively you can use ash (as with the traditional invocation: 'Even Ash, I do thee pluck, hoping thus to meet good luck') or hazel, since hazel nuts are symbolic of growth and wisdom. If you prefer to stay within the realm of lore, these woods are the most appropriate, though I stress that the power of the talisman is dependent on what effects the user brings to it.

This brings me to my next point, since talismans are traditionally made at the correct and 'auspicious' moment, usually when the apposite astrological configuration is present in the heavens. For your talisman this need be nothing more than the time of the waxing moon, preferably on its sixth day (approaching the first quarter) after the new moon. (The time of the waxing moon should be easy enough to discover; most good newspapers note the lunar phases in their weather section.) As we have seen, Pliny says the Druids cut mistletoe from the sacred oak at this time, and whether or not one believes in such notions as performing spells at the right time, the symbolism is vital. Here then, the feminine power of the moon, the goddess of the Unconscious realms, is waxing, is dynamic; she is in the process of gathering her strength. In short, she is now at her most powerful.

Now cut your chosen wood into a circle about 5 cm (2 in) in diameter – the wood should not be too thick – and sand it smooth on both sides. Then carefully carve the design shown on page 134 on to one side: reading clockwise from the middle stem at the top, it spells out the name of the goddess in Ogham, beginning with the primal 'b'.

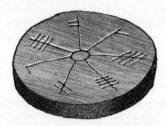

The other side of your talisman should bear the initial letters of your first name and surname: include your middle name if you normally use it in your signature. (Alternatively, you can reduce it to its corresponding numerological value.) Beneath these letters, inscribe a brief invocation for good luck: I suggest a Latin-style inscription as being practical and appropriate. Firstly, Roman inscriptions are written as initial letters, so you'll save space on your talisman. Secondly, remember that much Celtic culture and religion was absorbed by the Romans; an example of such cross-fertilisation can be found in the dedication to Sulis Minerva (at Bath), who seems to have superseded a former Celtic goddess, Brighid. Since this is to be a talisman for general good luck, a brief acknowledgement of the Goddess or some pithy aphorism will do. You can carve in the initial letters of any of the following Latin phrases, or construct your own:

*Ave Regina Caelorum (Hail, Queen of Heaven)*
*Fortuna Favet Fortibus (Fortune favours the brave)*
*Bonis Avibus (Under favourable signs)*
*Magnum Bonum (A great good)*
*Fide et Fiducia (By faith and confidence)*

When your carving is complete, concentrate your energies into the Wheel by visualisation, to ensure your talisman is magically charged. Visualise a shaft of light entering the talisman, for example. You can then carry the talisman or wear it. If you want to wear it, make a small hole in the top of the Wheel and thread a piece of leather or cord through it.

Brighid's role as the patroness of poetry or bardic lore is symbolised in her name carved on your talisman in Ogham script; her role elsewhere (at Oimelc or Imbolc) is to usher in the promise of light, growth, new potential and opportunity.

## The lorica of St Patrick

*'I arise today*
*Through the strength of heaven:*
*Light of sun,*
*Radiance of moon,*
*Splendour of fire ...'*

These are the opening words of St Patrick's lorica, or 'breastplate', a special form of protective invocation developed by the Irish Celts. It is largely irrelevant that these words were probably not written until about 300 years after the real fifth-century Irish saint lived, since what concerns us here is the very formation of the words and their role in modern magic.

The lorica has passed into modern Christianity as:

*'I bind unto myself today*
*The strong name of the Trinity.'*

Again the form of words is important; indeed, there are definite occult reasons why this should be so. Firstly, specific invocations or affirmations are part and parcel of magical practice in general; whether spoken or written, they are yet another 'tool' for influencing and impressing the mind. The emotional response is also important, so the actual choice of words is a key to the efficacy of a lorica or blessing. The following example shows why the form is vital.

So often individuals turn to magic because of bad luck, hoping to put things right via the occult. They are therefore approaching the subject from lack; this is always a dangerous condition, virtually guaranteed to make the magic fail. For it is not enough merely to want something (no matter how intensely); one must truly believe it can come true. There is another condition, too: you must consider the desire already realised! This is absolutely essential to this kind of magic, and much easier to write about than to achieve. The Universal Mind aspect of the Unconscious (where the magic takes place, as it were) is a living sphere of continuous creation: here there is no time, it is an eternal Now (just as, say, vivid dreams and memories have an intense 'nowness' about them). It follows that any desire projected as a future wish, with implications of doubt and uncertainty, will fail to invoke the correct 'response' from the Unconscious. Any magical technique geared to attracting goals should proceed on the basis of this 'now', a positive statement transmitted to the Unconscious as a *fait accompli,* as it were.

## Create your own lorica

It could be said that a modern version of the lorica is Emile Coué's auto-suggestive 'Every day, in every way, I am getting better and better.' Notice 'I am', an affirmatory statement based on nothing more than pure faith. I suggest you create your own lorica, with the emphasis on a positive statement about what is, not what you hope to achieve, while invoking the protection of a 'higher' force.

For example, you might use the first part of St Patrick's lorica: 'I arise today through the strength of heaven', and then construct short, affirmative lines about what you would like to happen in your life. The form of words is very important, so use carefully chosen, meaningful ones. If your choice of words does not invoke an appropriate emotional response in you, there is little chance of success.

Make your lorica fairly brief, for you need to recite it each morning when you get up. Copy it out neatly on a piece of parchment (or paper will do) and hang it somewhere you will see it.

Repetition is the other key to success, but what matters is that your lorica has the ability to 'charge' the Unconscious, to unearth its potential magic. This theme was covered by the occultist Eliphas Levi, who wrote of 'becoming a magnet' to attract one's desire, since, 'when he shall become sufficiently magnetic, let him be assured that the thing will come of itself, and without thinking of it'. Though much of this may sound simplistic, the 'transmission' of your desires to the Universal Mind is the real task. Hence the correct choice and structure of words, and the daily repetitions. You may like to end your lorica by saying aloud an old Roman statement of faith, which affirms your 'belief in belief itself'. It goes: *'credo quia absurdum est'* (I believe it because it is unreasonable). It is no different in kind from the amen – 'so be it' – said at the end of Christian prayers.

## Earth spirits

The magical activitity that follows is derived from traditional occult lore regarding the four elemental kingdoms (related to their symbolic objects in the four Tarot suits, or the gifts of the Tuatha dé Danaan we met in Chapter 2). The elemental spirits said to inhabit these kingdoms are Salamanders (Fire), Sylphs (Air), Ondines (Water) and Gnomes (Earth). They are related to the ethereal faery folk of Celtic legend, who – far from the popular idea of fairies as tiny, gossamer-winged creatures – are the same size and shape as human beings. Their natural realm is, however, the Otherworld, that place of beauty, wonder and perfection, and they therefore represent our 'link' to the magical world. In the words of scholar J.C. Cooper, they inhabit an 'intermediate realm, a strange mixture of the natural and supernatural', and are found in Celtic myth, 'under water, in wells, fountains and springs'.

The Earth Spirits have many names because of the different places they inhabit: they include elves, brownies, gnomes, hobgoblins (à la Robin Hood), trolls, pixies and leprechauns. In traditional lore, help from fairies – whether in growing crops, in successful animal births, or for a general increase in material goods – can be summoned by leaving a gift of some kind on a suitable altar. Tony Willis, in *Magick and the Tarot,* says:

*'The Earth Spirits connected with monetary gains … had an altar that was roughly round, like a coin. The appropriate offering for this type of spirit, naturally enough, is money.'*

Some readers may not like the idea of fairies and offering them gifts on an altar, yet the occult principle underlying the ceremony – as you give, so shall you receive – pervades the life of each individual on the planet, and does not apply only to material objects. It is certainly true that we reap what we sow on all levels of life; in occult theory this may be described as the Law of Attraction. Each cause has its corresponding effect, each action a corresponding reaction; the basic law in terms of material increase states that the 'giving' must happen first.

**Hooded Ones**

## *Offer gifts to the earth spirits*

Tony Willis suggests that you place a gift (of some value to you) to the Earth Spirits on a round stone for an increase in wealth or possessions. The gift could be a small piece of jewellery, a ring or even a pound coin, placed in a secluded glade or wood, accompanied by a thanksgiving for the increased wealth that is already on its way.

Then you must forget about it entirely. Whatever the ritual accompaniment, the magical 'attitude' must be correct. Magic works on the basis of your own belief; it is no use performing the ritual if you do not engage in it wholeheartedly. Nor must you worry about someone finding your offering and taking it, for that would miss the point. Of course, you need not believe in Earth Spirits, either: your 'gift' is a form of energy representing a certain kind of value to you; later on it will be exchanged for another kind of energy. Returning energy comes back increased.

Celtic votive offerings perform this function, whether you drop a few coins into a wishing well or offer something of greater value to the universe by casting gifts into a pool or stream, following the action with an appropriate thanksgiving. Here again, the act represents you giving out positive energies into the world. Again I stress that the right mental attitude is important: you are not performing this act with specific notions of increase; your first and only consideration is your donation, what you have to offer. You may add a blessing, knowing that 'the bread you have cast upon the waters will return tenfold', for this is quite different from wanting its return. Your increased wealth is a matter of faith, which your votive offering positively affirms. It is a paradox that desire must be removed from the equation. As the Victorian philosopher Austin Spare expressed so succinctly: 'Desire nothing and there is nothing you shall not realise.'

## A journey to the Otherworld: a guided visualisation

*'It is familiar to all men, both young and old, is found in the country, in the village, in the town, in all things created by God; yet it is despised by all. Rich and poor handle it every day. It is cast into the street by serving maids. Children play with it. Yet no one prizes it, though, next to the human soul, it is the most beautiful and precious thing on earth, and has the power to pull down kings and princes.'*

Robert Valens Rugl, *The Glory of the World*

What follows is a kind of guided visualisation, but I have presented it in the form of ancient Celtic story-telling, which we have discussed earlier. Memorise its main features and narrative (but allow your imagination to add whatever other elements seem appropriate). Then find a quiet time and place, when you are totally relaxed and know you will not be disturbed, and you can start your journey to the Otherworld

You may like to use some gentle music as a 'soundtrack' as the inner images unfold. You can buy recordings of numerous 'New Age' compositions, but however you prefer to work, there must be a deep sense of feeling and 'living' the material, as you react to whatever happens. One of the purposes of the journey is to invoke your intuitive responses – not from the mind, but from the heart – and as such the journey can be described as a kind of gentle initiation. However, the journey and the images you encounter comprise a 'mystery document' that you must 'solve' for yourself. As you first 'read through it' to digest the images, you will be 'asked' certain questions, asked to absorb certain mysteries; this relates to the unnamed 'substance' in the quote from Rugl above. The 'answer' (which will appear according to your level of understanding) is not the end of the matter, however. For although it can be stated simply, its many implications are the beginnings of wisdom.

So let your journey begin:

The sun is high in the sky as you walk towards the edge of a circular lake at whose centre is a high, flat-topped mound on an island. At the lake edge stand two fine silver birches, only a metre apart. As you approach these trees, you stand between them and extend each arm to touch their barks. As you gaze out on to the calm, clear lake, a silver branch appears mysteriously at your feet, and you retrieve it, placing it in your left hand. Then suddenly there is a green mist approaching you from the lake, which becomes so thick you cannot see anything else. The green mist before your eyes grows dark and as it clears you realise night has fallen.

Before you a glass boat awaits your presence at the shore; inside sits a silent young boatman dressed in a purple tunic fringed with gold. Holding a lantern with his left hand, he beckons with the other hand and you take your place in the boat, which turns to gleaming bronze as you step into it. You look at the boatman; he smiles and puts a finger to his lips. Unaware yet of the purpose of your journey, you disembark as the boatman gestures to a doorway made of oak in the side of the mound, on which pale moonlight shines from above. As you make a path to the doorway, it opens instantly and there, out of the gloom, stands a lame old man who has been expecting you. As you cross the threshold and the door closes behind you, you are aware of a dazzling light as you stand in the banqueting hall of a great royal palace. On the long oak table there is an array of fine wine and food, with 13 places laid: six down each side, and one at the table head, for a guest as yet unknown to the royal household.

In one corner, facing south, stands a bubbling cauldron full of honey-coloured liquid; it is said that each year three drops of divine wisdom can be tasted from it. In the other corner, facing north, stands a carved block of stone, on which it is said kings have been crowned. In the corner that faces east, a magnificent red-tipped spear rests against the wall; opposite, in the west, is a gleaming, unsheathed silver sword that can cut through any object you care to mention. Then a finely dressed bard appears and shows you a vision of a silver casket in the shape of a woman's head. Inside it, you are told, is an object whose power has caused miracles and riches to occur, should anyone understand its purpose.

Then the vision disappears, along with the bard, and the goddess Sovereignty is enthroned at the head of the feasting table. Of regal bearing, she is flame haired, clothed in a cape of fine red silk and has a golden torque at her neck. Wordlessly, she tells you more about the enigmatic object the bard said was hidden inside the silver reliquary. Though she does not speak, you hear her words as she relates the wondrous qualities of this object. It is, you learn, a pearl of great value, the stone of the wise and the fruit of the blessed to all that have come by it. This object has travelled among kings and peasants alike, among the learned and the fools, and nothing on earth could prove of better fortune, such is its capacity to produce wealth. Above all, it is the key to the hidden mysteries of life itself, for inside the object lie all the secrets of the universe.

From inside her cape she produces this very object and places it on the table before you. She silently bids you to open it and receive its secret, for you are the expected one. Your eyes fall upon it: it is a simple, small, black wooden box, rather scuffed and dirty, the hinges rusted as if its previous owner had neglected it. Quietly, you lift the lid and there is nothing there but a small square of red silk, beneath which lies a silver coin.

When you catch your reflection in the silver, however, everything becomes perfectly clear to you and you smile knowingly.

Then you are back in your usual, everyday surroundings, and you open your eyes. And here, perhaps, you smile once more. [end of guided visualisation]

# Conclusion:
# *The Celtic Twilight*

The National Portrait Gallery in Edinburgh has an unusual painting. St Columba stands among a group of Picts, the Christian cross raised in his right hand. The humble saint is in sixth-century Scotland, in a rocky stronghold, to convert Brude mac Maelchon (Bridei), the northern ruler of these indigenous folk.

That this conversion exists only on the fringes of known history need not concern us. What is strange about the painting is in its detail. Brude sits on a square, granite plinth that is decorated with ninth-century knotwork; his cape is fastened by the so-called Hunterston brooch, a relic of the eighth century. Behind the saint, one of his attendants holds a hooked staff, a crozier of the type common in medieval Ireland; behind Brude stands his wife, a stern-faced Victorian-looking matriarch. The latter is not surprising, for the painting (by William Hole, b. 1845) is an example of the Victorian 'Celtic' revival, an artistic 'renaissance' that sought to recreate our idealised, legendary past.

Some commentators, however, take exception to such chocolate-box representations. Writer Lloyd Laing complains, for example, that the literature of W.B. Yeats' Celtic Twilight movement is just a romantic gloss on the primary material, 'in which a group of nineteenth-century poets tried to create a new Celtic literature without any real understanding of the original'. Further, he says:

> '... the "Celtic" art sold today in craft shops is ... all too
> often inspired by Norse rather than Celtic imagery.
> It is not a traditional craft but a conscious revival,
> geared entirely to a tourist market.'

What Laing says is true as far as it goes, and no doubt the same comments about 'conscious revival' would apply to the neo-paganism and 'old religion' of today's Wicca. However, any culture reinterprets its mythological past not only on the basis of available written records, however fragmentary, but also according to how its viewpoint has been coloured by its own intellectual or emotional values. In other words, we impose our own imagination on the mythical past, sometimes with little regard for history, and adapt its traditions through contemporary understanding. This is just as it should be; it is human nature and so there cannot be any other way, even with 'Celtic art sold today in craft shops'.

What matters, however, is that there is a relationship to our ancient culture, though it is foolish to insist on the 'correct', authentic reading of myth or pseudo-history. The psychological interpretations I have offered in this book are not the only way of exposing their 'truths'. They are, of course, aimed at the contemporary reader and our contemporary culture.

So what relevance might Celtic religious and spiritual ideas have for today's 'seeker'? The Celtic path is a path of the heart, the search for the Grail, the spirit of adventure and longing for the Otherworld, all of which lead inexorably to the Goddess. Since this is essentially a Feminine path presided over by the Mother Goddess, the spirit of Celtic myth reminds us of our essential nature and the 'place' we came from, for the womb and the thread of Fate are one and the same.

Contemporary culture, however, is essentially 'masculine': actively goal-oriented, competitive and concerned with 'progress' and acquisition, whether of status, knowledge or money. We are also living in an ever-faster world, where (helped by technology and fed by electronic media) we demand instant gratification for our desires; quality must bow before quantity. So many people seem to be running faster and faster to stay in the same place, yet many others feel we have forgotten our true goals. Whether we define these as ancient truths or the wisdom of the Feminine, it is not the gifts of the heart and soul that are valued today, but those of the mind and body.

We have seen how many Celtic heroes must win the help of the Goddess in their quests, for the mythical journey always secretly leads back to the Self, fate, or that which we truly are. The story paraphrased below about the goddess Rhiannon and her pursuer Pwyll can be read on various levels and you can, of course, find your own 'truth' in this subtle tale, but I feel it has much to say about our modern 'masculine' ego-quest for individual 'progress' which, in the end, is always a quest for personal happiness. As Pwyll and his men chase after the goddess, he learns that he need only call out her name to achieve his goal; that to make progress, he must stop running. We are all like Pwyll, rushing to keep up when, paradoxically, we already secretly possess the far more valuable goal.

## Pwyll, Prince of Dyfed

Pwyll, Prince of Dyfed, was at Aberth, his chief palace, where a great feast had been prepared for him and his men. After the first course, however, Pwyll left to sit on a mound above the palace; it is said that no one could go there without being witness to a wonder. As Pwyll and his men sat on top of the mound, they saw a woman on a pure white horse, her garments shining with the gold of the sun. The horse was moving slowly and seemed to be approaching the foot of the mound.

Pwyll was curious and ordered one of his men to go and ask the woman's name, but as the man went to meet her by the side of the road she passed by. He tried to run after her, but the faster he ran, the further she seemed to move away. So he returned to his master, saying it was useless to follow her on foot. 'Then go into the palace,' said Pwyll, 'find the fastest horse there, and then find this lady.'

The man did as he was ordered. Even though he used spurs on his horse, the faster he went, the further she got away from him. So he returned to Pwyll again with the same bad news.

'I suspect some illusion here,' said Pwyll. The next day they did the same thing and went up on to the mound after the first course of the meal. The prince ordered another young man to take the swiftest horse from the field and, as they waited, they saw the same lady on the same horse. 'Now,' ordered Pwyll, 'here is the same lady from yesterday. Go after her and find out who she is.' She did not ride past them very quickly, so the young man set off at a pace he thought would allow him to quickly overtake her. Still she remained out of reach; however much the young man urged on his horse, the same distance lay between him and the lady.

So the following day, as Pwyll took his men to climb the mound again, he ordered that his own horse be saddled. After a little while the woman appeared. 'I see her coming,' said Pwyll. However, just as his companions had before, the prince could come no nearer to the enigmatic lady, even when riding at the fastest speed he could. At last, exasperated, he called out: 'Dear lady, for the sake of him you love best, stay for me.' 'I will stay with pleasure,' she replied, 'and it would have been better for your horse had you asked before.'

Then she drew back her veil and looked him in the eyes. Pwyll spoke first: 'Lady, where do you come from, and where are you going?' 'I am engaged on my own errand,' she answered, 'and I am glad to see you.' Pwyll saw that she was very beautiful, more radiant that any other woman he had ever seen. He asked who she was. 'I am Rhiannon,' she replied, 'the daughter of Hefeydd the Old.' The prince offered his greetings and again wondered why this beautiful stranger rode past the same place each day. 'Lady,' he said, 'will you tell me the purpose of these journeys?' 'I will tell you,' she replied, 'for my main quest was to seek out no one but you.'

# Further Reading

Barber, Richard, *Myths and Legends of the British Isles,* Boydell, 1999

Bord, Janet and Colin, *Mysterious Britain,* Paladin, 1974

Carr-Gomm, Philip, *The Druid Way,* Element Books, 1993

Chadwick, Nora, *The Celts,* Penguin, 1991

Conway, David, *Magic: an Occult Primer,* Granada, 1974

Cooper, Quentin, and Sullivan, Paul, *Maypoles, Martyrs and Mayhem,* Bloomsbury, 1995

Delaney, Frank, *The Celts,* HarperCollins, 1993

Eliade, Mircea, *A History of Religious Ideas,* Collins, 1979

Hartley, Christine, *The Western Mystery Tradition,* Aquarian Press, 1986

Hope, Murry, *Practical Celtic Magic,* Aquarian Press, 1987

Laing, Lloyd, *Celtic Britain,* Routledge & Kegan Paul/BCA, 1979

Matthews, Caitlin, *Elements of the Celtic Tradition,* Element Books, 1989

Matthews, John, *Elements of The Arthurian Tradition,* Element Books, 1989

Matthews, John (ed.), *At the Table of the Grail – Magic and the Use of the Imagination,* Arkana, 1987

Matthews, John, and Green, Marian, *The Grail Seeker's Companion,* Aquarian Press, 1986

Pennick, Nigel, *Practical Magic in the Northern Tradition,* Aquarian Press, 1989

Rolleston, T.W., *Celtic Myths and Legends,* Senate, 1994

Stewart, R.J., *Celtic Gods, Celtic Goddesses,* Blandford, 1990

Stewart, R.J., *Merlin Tarot,* Thorsons, 1992

Tolstoi, Nikolai, *The Quest for Merlin,* Hamish Hamilton, 1985

Toulson, Shirley, *The Celtic Year,* Element Books, 1993

Willis, Tony, *Magick and the Tarot,* Aquarian Press, 1988

Yeats, W.B., *The Celtic Twilight,* Prism Press, 1990

# Index

Index